S-3 Viking

Written by Brad Elward

In Action®

NK
05
0583
NK
705
USS CONSTELLATION
NAVY
VS-37

Squadron Signal®
Publications

Cover Art by Don Greer

Line Illustrations by Todd Sturgell

(Front Cover) Two Air Anti-Submarine Squadron Thirty (VS-30) *Diamondcutters* highlight the Viking's considerable anti-ship capability. *Diamond 704* (BuNo. 159769) carries a CATM-65E Maverick on wing station five (W5) while *Diamond 706* (BuNo. 160606) in the background carries a CATM-84K SLAM. Designed to combat Soviet submarines, the S-3 became a dominant sea control and surveillance platform. (Jose Ramos)

(Back Cover) A VS-35 S-3B holds the distinction of being the only carrier aircraft to transport a sitting United States President. On 1 May 2003, President George W. Bush flew aboard USS *Abraham Lincoln* (CVN-72) to mark the end of large unit combat operations in Operation Iraqi Freedom. The *Blue Wolves* designated the aircraft NAVY 1 in the tradition of marking the official Presidential aircraft. (United States Navy)

About the In Action® Series

In Action® books, despite the title of the genre, are books that trace the development of a single type of aircraft, armored vehicle, or ship from prototype to the final production variant. Experimental or "one-off" variants can also be included. Our first *In Action*® book was printed in 1971.

 Hardcover ISBN **978-0-89747-701-7**
Softcover ISBN 978-0-89747-702-4
Proudly printed in the U.S.A.
Copyright 2012 Squadron/Signal Publications
1115 Crowley Drive, Carrollton, TX 75006-1312 U.S.A.

Military/Combat Photographs and Snapshots

If you have any photos of aircraft, armor, soldiers, or ships of any nation, particularly wartime snapshots, why not share them with us and help make Squadron/Signal's books all the more interesting and complete in the future? Any photograph sent to us will be copied and returned. Electronic images are preferred. The donor will be fully credited for any photos used. Please send them to:

Squadron/Signal Publications
1115 Crowley Drive
Carrollton, TX 75006-1312 U.S.A.
www.SquadronSignalPublications.com

(Title Page) VS-37 originated from a reserve unit, VS-871, was officially designated an Air Anti-Submarine Squadron 37. (VS-37) in 1953. The *Sawbucks* deployed aboard USS *Constellation* (CV-64) with Carrier Air Wing 9 (CVW-9) in the mid 1970s and again in the mid-1980s as part of CVW-14. The squadron flew Electronic Surveillance Missions (ESM) from USS *Independence* (CV-60) from August through December 1990, but did not participate in Operation Desert Storm. VS-37 disestablished in March 1995. (The Tail Hook Association via Author)

Acknowledgments

Special thanks to Commodore Phil Voss, USN (Ret); Dr. Hill Goodspeed; Captain Evan B. Piritz, former Commodore, Sea Control Wing Atlantic Fleet; CDR Chris Schenck, former Chief of Staff, Sea Control Wing, Atlantic; CDR Robin Higgs, Sea Control Wing Weapons School CIC; David Reade, P-3 Publications; Captain Danny Power, USN (Ret.); CW04 Eric "Wally" Wobler, USN (Ret.); LCDR Richard B. Burgess, USN (Ret); James Meyer, Lockheed Martin Aircraft Company; Kenneth Katz.

An ES-3A Shadow from VQ-5 flies in formation with an S-3B from VS-41 off the coast of Southern California. The ES-3A performed electronic warfare (EW) and signal intelligence (SIGINT) missions and operated from 1991 until it was withdrawn from service in 1999. VQ-5 was stationed at Naval Air Station (NAS) North Island, California, although it maintained a permanently forward-deployed two-plane detachment, Det 5, with Fleet Air Reconnaissance Squadron 5 (CVW-5) at Naval Air Facility (NAF) Misawa, Japan. Shadow 720 (BuNo. 159403) has its Forward Looking Infrared Radar (FLIR) unit deployed. (CAPT Chris Buhlmann, USNR)

Introduction to Carrier-Based ASW

The use of aircraft for long-range anti-submarine patrols dates back to World War I, when the U.S. flew land-based Curtis H.12 aircraft on maritime reconnaissance missions to counter the German threat. Despite these American efforts, German submarines wreaked havoc on Allied shipping, sinking over 11 million tons over the course of the conflict. It was in World War II that carrier-based anti-submarine warfare (ASW) made its debut. ASW efforts in both the Atlantic and Pacific Theaters were dominated by American and British escort carriers (CVE) flying Grumman Wildcats and Avengers. The ASW Avengers carried rockets, bombs, and 350-lb depth charges and were equipped with a wing-affixed radome-mounted ASD-1 radar (designated TBF/TBM-1Ds) Avenger-laden CVEs were deployed to combat German Unterseeboot (U-boat) packs in the so-called Mid-Atlantic Gap, the region in the middle of the Atlantic beyond the reach of land-based ASW aircraft, and in the Pacific to protect shipping and landing forces. The CVEs destroyed 53 German U-boats and 11 Japanese submarines.

The U.S. Navy refined its carrier-based anti-submarine efforts in the post-war years, deploying ASW hunter-killer air units based on the Grumman Avenger-derived TBM-3W Hunter (Guppy) and TBM-3S Killer (Scrapper) aircraft. Two aircraft were used because the Avenger airframe was too small to carry all of the sensor equipment and weaponry necessary to detect, track, and attack submarines. During the early 1950s, the Avenger teams were replaced with the team of more potent and purpose-built Grumman AF Guardian AF-2W (Hunter) and AF-2S (Killer), which prevailed until the Grumman S2F Tracker (redesignated the S-2 in 1962) replaced both.

The Tracker was the first single aircraft airframe designed from the outset to perform the ASW mission. It represented a significant leap in capabilities over the hunter/killer Guardian combination. The S-2 brought together both missions and carried surface

An S-3A of VS-21 (BuNo. 159402) flies in formation with a Grumman S-2G Tracker from VS-37. The Viking replaced the Tracker as the Navy's carried-based ASW aircraft beginning in 1974. VS-21 was the first fleet squadron to receive the S-3A. The *Fighting Red Tails* made their first carrier deployment from July 1975 through January 1976 aboard USS *John F. Kennedy* (CV-67) The aircraft wears the high-visibility markings prevalent in the 1970s and 1980s, as well as the squadron's "Viking" logo. (Robert Lawson Collection)

search radar, electronic sensors, a retractable Magnetic Anomaly Detection (MAD) boom, and an acoustic suite with sonobuoys for search and tracking submarines, as well as torpedoes, bombs, and depth charges for completing the kill. The Tracker entered U.S. Navy service in February 1954 and was deployed aboard dedicated ASW carriers (World War II Era *Essex*-Class carriers redesignated as CVS), operating in independent ASW Task Forces protecting the larger Attack Carrier (CVA) Strike Forces and clearing sea-lanes for merchant shipping. The CVS typically deployed with two Tracker squadrons and a single Sikorsky HSS-1 Seabat (redesignated the SH-34) and later the Sikorsky SH-3 Sea King helicopter squadron.

As the Cold War intensified, the need arose for an even more advanced ASW platform to counter the increasingly capable Soviet submarine fleet, which by the early 1960s included new classes of quieter nuclear-powered vessel. such as the Soviet Project 658 (NATO designation "Hotel"), Project 627 *Kit* (NATO designation "November"), and Project 675 (NATO designation "Echo-II class"). These vessels threatened the U.S. Navy's ability to project power and protect trans-Atlantic shipping lanes crucial to the defense of Europe. The Navy therefore sought a follow-on platform to the Tracker, which could meet these emerging threats and provide the same capabilities as the new land-based Lockheed P-3A Orion.

The Navy considered eliminating all carrier-based ASW aircraft as well as the CVS fleet, and opting for a larger fleet of land-based P-3 Orions but abandoned the idea because there were considerable regions where even the long-range Orion could not reach. Orions were also dependent on the availability of land bases, which were not available in certain regions. With a new fleet of ASW carriers out of reach due to cost considerations, the Navy turned its attention to a Tracker replacement that could be deployed aboard Strike Carriers as part of the new carrier air wing concept that incorporated the ASW aircraft into the traditional strike air wing.

The resulting aircraft program produced the S-3A Viking, the most capable carrier-based ASW aircraft ever built. The Viking represented a quantum leap in capability over the Tracker and introduced the first digital computer system merging the aircraft's various sensors and weapons systems. The S-3A was followed in 1987 by the even more capable S-3B, which introduced an advanced sonobuoy and an improved ESM suite, the AGM-84 Harpoon air-to-surface missile, and the sophisticated Inverse Synthetic Aperture Radar (ISAR), and which made the Viking the dominant carrier-based sea control platform.

The S-3B was joined in 1991 by the ES-3A Shadow, which quickly established itself as a superior carrier-based electronic surveillance platform. The Shadow gave the Carrier Battle Group Commander an organic electronic intelligence (ELINT) and signal intelligence (SIGINT) capability vastly superior to the EA-3B Whale that it replaced. First deployed in 1993, a detachment of two Shadows operated with each carrier air wing (CVW) until the aircraft's retirement in late 1999.

Since the S-3B's ASW gear was removed in 1999, the Viking's main roles have been surface surveillance and aerial refueling. The Viking's end began in late 2003, when the Navy unveiled its Sundown Plan, outlining the aircraft's retirement schedule. The last S-3 squadron, East Coast based VS-22's *Checkmates,* was disestablished in January 2009.

A VS-38 S-3A Viking rests on the tarmac with wings folded, during a period when the squadron was assigned to Air Wing 14 aboard USS *Enterprise* (CVN-65). The world-famous *Red Griffins* were the last squadron to deploy with the S-3A. (Naval Aviation Museum)

The Viking production run consisted of 187 S-3A aircraft manufactured in seven Lots. Here, the final S-3A produced (BuNo. 160607) sits on the tarmac at Lockheed's Palmdale facility in California in the summer of 1978. A Lockheed P-3 Orion can be seen in the background. (Robert Lawson Collection)

The Grumman Avenger played a vital role in the United States Navy anti-submarine warfare effort during World War II and the late 1940s. The Avenger (designated TBF/ TBM-1Ds) deployed in two-plane detachments; one aircraft performed the search operations, using the wing-affixed radome-mounted ASD-1 radar, and the second aircraft carried the offensive capability, using rockets, bombs, and 350-lb depth charges. (Robert Lawson Collection)

Among these six Vikings, *Diamond 705* carries an Aero-1D droppable fuel tank on wing station 6 (W6), emblazed with a "T" for "Texaco," to signify the aircraft's mission as the air wing tanker. The emblem on the nose radome states, "Defending Freedom to the Very Last Day: 1953-2005." VS-30, which deployed from USS *Saratoga* (CV-60) during Operation Desert Storm, disestablished at NAS Jacksonville, Florida, on 20 April 2007. (Jose Ramos)

Aircraft Development

By the late 1950s and early 1960s, the Navy had undertaken a series of internal studies to investigate a carrier-based follow-on to the piston-engine Grumman S2F Tracker. The Navy evaluated fixed-wing aircraft, VSTOL/STOL aircraft, and helicopters, as well as a variety of power plant alternatives.

The VSX (heavier-than-air antisubmarine aircraft, experimental) concept began to circulate in June 1964 as the Navy intensified its quest for a successor to the Tracker. The concept sought a more capable ASW platform, fitted with advanced weaponry and sensors, and possessing greater range, endurance, and speed than the S2F Tracker. Earlier studies had recommended a conventional aircraft with twin turbofan engines. One of the primary goals of VSX was to enable the carriers to find and attack submarines far enough away from the task force so as to prevent the submarine from launching a torpedo or missile.

A Special Operational Requirement (SOR) was drawn up in 1966 and a formal Request for Proposal (RFP) was issued in late 1968. Six companies responded to the RFP, including Grumman Corporation, which had produced the Avenger, Guardian, and Tracker ASW aircraft; and Lockheed Martin, which had significant land-based experience with the PV-1/2 Ventura, P-2 Neptune, and P-3 Orion, but little experience with carrier aircraft. Other companies submitting proposals included Ling-Temco-Vought (LTV) Aerospace Corporation (manufacturer of the carrier-based A-7 Corsair II and F-8 Crusader), North American, General Dynamics, and Douglas. A seven-month project

Rockwell was one of the manufacturers submitting a competing proposal during the VSX competition in the late 1960s. Its design featured a unique method of launching a torpedo from the left wing station. (Rockwell Aircraft via Carl Altevogt)

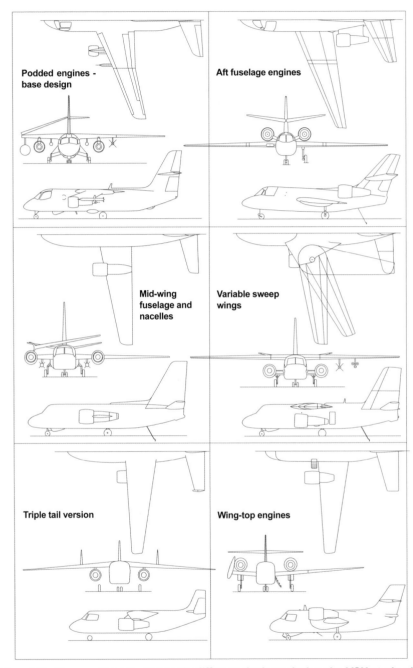

Podded engines - base design

Aft fuselage engines

Mid-wing fuselage and nacelles

Variable sweep wings

Triple tail version

Wing-top engines

Lockheed Martin considered at least six different designs during the VSX study phase. The S-3A emerged from a variation of design one in the upper left, referenced as the "podded engines – base design." (Lockheed Martin)

study ensued, followed by an extensive contract definition phase wherein the various competing manufacturers were teamed into two groups, one headed by Grumman and the other by Lockheed.

Recognizing its lack of experience in carrier-based operations, Lockheed Martin teamed with LTV and UNIVAC Federal Systems Division of Sperry Rand, which was pursuing an integrated ASW processor suite. Grumman paired with the Convair Division of General Dynamics and IBM.

A separate contract had already been let to General Electric (GE) for the TF34 turbofan engine, following a similar competition with General Motors Corporation (Allison Division). The Navy had already been studying the then-new high-bypass turbofan, which General Electric had proposed for the Air Force-sponsored Lockheed C-5 Galaxy transport. The Navy believed that in the proper power class, the turbofan technology would be suitable for the VSX.

In October 1965, the Navy narrowed its consideration for a VSX engine to an 8,000-lb-9,000-lb-thrust turbofan or a 3,500-shp turboprop. After considering a derivative of the Allison T78-A-2 regenerative turboprop, the Navy eventually rejected the concept because the engine could not meet VSX mission requirements and aircraft speed.

In May 1966, the Navy formally issued to the engine industry a Request for Quotation (RFQ) for a 14-month Advanced Engine Development Program. The United Aircraft Company, Curtis-Wright Corporation, Allison, and GE submitted proposals, and in June 1967, the Navy selected designs by GE and Allison for a final competition. GE's proposal, the TF-34-GE-2, was submitted in January 1968 and was derived from the TF64/F1 gas generator with a high-bypass fan. The Navy gave GE a contract to develop

VS-41 *Shamrocks* received the first S-3A Vikings and served as the West Cost Fleet Replacement Squadron (FRS) until it closed its doors in the mid-2000s. This Viking, BuNo. 159417, wears high-visibility markings and has the Modex NJ 752. (Michael Grove)

The S-3A prototype drawing submitted by Lockheed shows a strong resemblance to the actual S-3A as designed. The most notable difference is the cockpit canopy area, which appears larger in the drawing, and the larger crew window. (Robert Lawson Collection)

YS-3A No. 1 (BuNo. 157992) takes its maiden flight on 21 January 1972 with a Grumman F9F Cougar chase plane trailing behind. This Viking served as the primary flight test aircraft, evaluating the S-3A's flying characteristics and power plant performance. (Robert Lawson Collection)

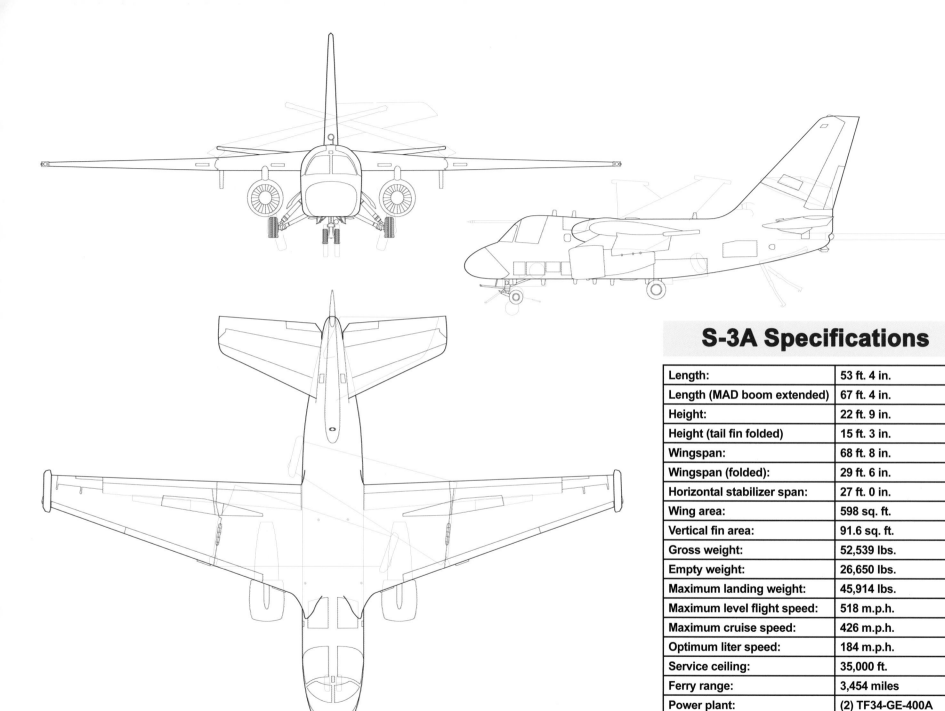

S-3A Specifications

Length:	53 ft. 4 in.
Length (MAD boom extended)	67 ft. 4 in.
Height:	22 ft. 9 in.
Height (tail fin folded)	15 ft. 3 in.
Wingspan:	68 ft. 8 in.
Wingspan (folded):	29 ft. 6 in.
Horizontal stabilizer span:	27 ft. 0 in.
Wing area:	598 sq. ft.
Vertical fin area:	91.6 sq. ft.
Gross weight:	52,539 lbs.
Empty weight:	26,650 lbs.
Maximum landing weight:	45,914 lbs.
Maximum level flight speed:	518 m.p.h.
Maximum cruise speed:	426 m.p.h.
Optimum liter speed:	184 m.p.h.
Service ceiling:	35,000 ft.
Ferry range:	3,454 miles
Power plant:	(2) TF34-GE-400A turbofans 9,275 lbs. dry thrust

the TF34-GE-2 engine.

The Lockheed team evaluated several configurations for the VSX, all based around two General Electric TF34-GE-2 9,725-lbs thrust high-bypass-ratio turbofan engines. Consideration was given to mounting the engines in pods, either above or beneath the wings, on the lower sides of the fuselage, on the aft fuselage, or on wing-pylon nacelles. Engineers also studied the best configuration for the vertical tail surface, examining single and triple tail surfaces, and considered the possibility of using a variable-sweep wing design (like that used in the General Dynamics F-111 Aardvark and Grumman F-14 Tomcat), hoping to yield a higher transit speed while retaining the ability to loiter for long periods of time. The team settled on the final S-3A configuration of shoulder-mounted, folding wings, pod-mounted under-wing turbofan engines, and a tall vertical folding tail fin. Like its S-2 predecessor, the S-3A was to carry a crew of four.

Lockheed's design changed very little during the final stages of the competition. Among those changes, however, was a reduction of the wing quarter-chord sweepback angle from 20 degrees to 15 degrees in order to improve overall structural arrangement and balance. Wing area was also increased from 580 sq ft (53.9 sq m) to 598 sq ft (55.6 sq m). Finally, the Navy enlarged the folded span from 27 ft 6 in (8.38m) to 29 ft 6 in (8.99m), which meant relocation of the wing fold lines. Unfortunately, this change led to increased drag and a corresponding modification to the wing contour. On the positive side, though, the extra fuel capacity resulting from the wider folded span added some 20 percent more range and endurance to the original specifications.

On 1 August 1969 the Lockheed team was awarded a full-scale development fixed price-plus-incentives contract involving seven distinct production lots and contemplating 199 aircraft. Contingencies were built into the contract to permit a purchase of up to 310 aircraft. Production Lot 1 was to consist of six aircraft for flight tests and Lot 2 would consist of two research and development airframes – one for static/drop tests and one for fatigue testing. The contract, initially valued at $461 million, was almost immediately modified to add two additional airframes, bringing the contract value to a total of $494 million.

The Lockheed contract provided for initial funding of a specified number of test articles and then made further funding contingent upon the completion of significant milestones, such as a laboratory demonstration of integrated avionics systems, a successful first flight, Navy Preliminary Evaluation, a flying test-bed avionics assessment, and delivery of an aircraft ready for Board of Inspection and Survey (BIS) trials.

Design work on the Viking proceeded during 1969, with the S-3A mock-up receiving Navy approval in March 1970. Wind tunnel tests were also performed during late 1970 and early 1971 at Langley using its 16-foot Transonic Dynamic Tunnel. Spin and recovery evaluations were conducted in the 20-foot Vertical Spin Tunnel during 1972 with no resulting modifications.

On 8 November 1971, the S-3A formally received the name "Viking" during a rollout ceremony at Lockheed's Burbank facility. After some 13 million engineering man-hours of development, the first YS-3A Viking (BuNo. 157992) completed its initial taxi and systems trials at the Lockheed Air Terminal and was transported to Palmdale, California.

VS-31, an East Coast S-3A squadron, transitioned to the Viking in 1976. Here, BuNo. 159766 (AG 706) sits on the tarmac at NAS Norfolk in April 1978. (Stephen H. Miller)

The *Screwbirds* of VS-33 received their first S-3A in 1976 and took the Viking on cruise in October 1977. They operated the Alpha until 1992 when they transitioned to the more capable S-3B. (LCDR Richard Burgess, [Ret.])

Flight Tests

The first Viking took to the sky on 21 January 1972 ahead of schedule, with pilots John Christiansen and Lyle Schaefer at the controls. Although scheduled for a mere half hour hop, the flight lasted 102 minutes. The flight, conducted at the Palmdale facility, evaluated the aircraft's slow speed flight envelope, exploring speeds between 120 and 200 knots up to altitudes of 20,000 feet. The maiden flight checked the Viking's controls, engines, stall characteristics, and landing gear. Christiansen commented afterward that the aircraft "was exceptionally stable and very responsive to controls."

The aircraft's second flight occurred a few weeks later and expanded the flight envelope to 250 knots and introduced various banking maneuvers and low-G accelerations. The second flight test lasted 2 hours and 17 minutes. A third flight occurred on 11 February 1972, lasting 2 hours and 56 minutes and extending the flight envelope to 25,000 feet.

In August of 1971, Lockheed began tests of the Viking's avionics suite using an NP-3A Orion referred to as the S-3 Avionics Flying Test Bed. These tests accumulated 790 flight hours. Following the successful demonstration of the Viking's proposed avionics suite, the Navy confirmed the first production order of 13 S-3As at a price of $102.8 million. April also saw the start of the Navy's Preliminary Evaluations (NPE), the official flight test program; six Viking pilots participated in NPE-1, flying a total of 19 flights and 59 flight hours.

The S-3A is formally introduced to the Navy on 8 November 1971. The Viking represented the state-of-the-art in ASW capabilities. Of the 187 examples produced, 119 were later converted to S-3B standards and 16 were modified as ES-3A Shadows. Six S-3As were converted into a carrier onboard delivery (COD) variant, designated the US-3A. (Lockheed Martin Company)

The Viking's initial flight lasted 102 minutes. Flown by test pilot John Christianson and test co-pilot Lyle Schaefer, the flight took place some seven weeks ahead of schedule. By mid-February, YS-3A No. 1 had flown on three flights and logged six hours 55 minutes of flight time. (Lockheed Martin Company)

YS-3A No. 1 (BuNo. 157992) is restrained by the barrier net. It was later damaged in an Emergency Barrier Arrested Test at NAS Lakehurst, New Jersey. Although stricken from the inventory, it was later refurbished and is on display at NAS Jacksonville, Florida. (Robert Lawson Collection)

In May 1972 the Navy began its Navy Preliminary Assessment (NPA) of avionics, and further marked the successful completion of the avionics test bed segment, accumulating over 790 hours of flights with the P-3A flying test bed. A second NPA was conducted in November and a separate NPE 2 was completed a month prior. NPE-3 began in January 1973 and saw the first evaluation of a fully equipped S-3A in an operational setting. NPE-4 commenced in August 1973. The aircraft's success led to a $223 million contract for Lot 4 purchase of 35 aircraft. The Navy's Board of Inspection and Survey (BIS) trials (similar to the current Operational Evaluation [OpEval]) commenced in October 1973 and lasted six months, focusing on an "evaluation of the airframe, associated systems, and methods of future operations." BIS trials were completed on schedule on 21 March 1974, and the S-3A was approved for fleet service.

Carrier suitability trials took place in two phases, the latter concurrent with commencement of the BIS trials. In May 1973, the fourth test aircraft, BuNo. 157995, began a series of suitability trials at NAS Patuxent River. Actual "at sea" trials began aboard USS Forrestal (CV-59) off Virginia Capes on 26 November 1973. Sea trials were initially flown by the ninth S-3A (BuNo. 158861), which recorded the airframe's first carrier deck trap. A second Viking (YS-3A No. 4, BuNo. 157995) joined number 158861 and the two spent a week at sea, logging 58 catapult launches and arrested landings (seven

at night) and another 144 "touch-and-goes." Four of the touch-and-goes and one of the arrested landings were conducted on a single engine. Gross weights of up to 52,500 lbs (23,814kg) were tested.

Like many other aviation programs, each of the prototype aircraft was assigned to specific tasks.

Pre-production Aircraft
2999   Drop test/static test vehicle.
3000 S-3A   Static mock-up aircraft; later involved in S-3 Service Life Assessment Program (SLAP).
YS-3A No. 1 BuNo. 157992 – Evaluated the Viking's flying qualities and power plant performance.
YS-3A No. 2 BuNo. 157993 – Tested structural buildup, flight envelope expansion, and basic AFCS. Later used as in-flight refueling and stores separation test aircraft and as Skunk Works classified project.
YS-3A No. 3 BuNo. 157994 – First Viking equipped with a full ASW suite; used for avionics evaluations and demonstrations. This Viking conducted first successful tracking of a submerged submarine in August 1972.
YS-3A No. 4 BuNo. 157995 – Carrier suitability tests at NAS Patuxent River and

Seven Vikings, including prototypes 1, 2, 3, 5, 6, and 7, sit on the tarmac at the Naval Air Test Center, NAS Patuxent River, Maryland, in November 1973. The prototypes, plus one production aircraft (shown at the end of the flight line), were undergoing Navy Board of Inspection and Survey (BIS) trials, which included months of weapons system testing. The BIS trials were the last major development before delivering the aircraft to the fleet. (United States Navy via Richard Burgess, USN. [Ret.])

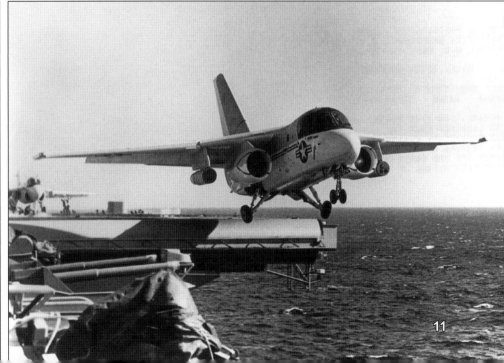

Viking 158861 makes the aircraft's first catapult launch from a carrier. The Viking conducted its first sea trials aboard USS Forrestal (CV-59) in November 1973. Viking 158861 (the ninth production aircraft) was later joined by Viking No. 4 (BuNo. 157995) and together they made 58 catapult launches and arrested landings. The carrier suitability tests were conducted off the Virginia coast. (United States Navy via Richard Burgess, USN. [Ret.])

The S-3A is manufactured at the Lockheed Martin facility in Burbank, California. Vought, one of the prime subcontractors, turned out the wing center section and the tail empennage at its Grand Prairie, Texas, plant, then transported the sections to Burbank for final assembly. (Lockheed Martin Company)

aboard USS *Forrestal* (CV-59)

YS-3A No. 5 BuNo. 157996 – Hydraulic, fuel, air conditioning, and avionics evaluations.

YS-3A No. 6 BuNo. 157997 – Some armament and weapons testing, and avionics integration tests.

YS-3A No. 7 BuNo. 157998 – Evaluated weapons systems, bombs, rockets, mines, and missiles.

YS-3A No. 8 BuNo. 159999 – Lost on 3 August 1973 during test flight.

The Viking flight test program lasted a total of 26 months and logged 2,600 flight hours. Overall, the flight test results correlated almost perfectly with calculated performances.

The two static articles were tested to evaluate the Viking's airframe fatigue. Aircraft 2999 was used as Vought's drop test vehicle and completed over 1,000 simulated carrier landings and a service lifetime of over 13,000 hours of wear on the S-3A's landing gear. Lockheed used Aircraft 3000 for its Lifetime Stress Simulation tests, putting the airframe through over two typical service lifetimes of fatigue. Data from these tests would later provide the basis for Lockheed's S-3 Finite Element Model (FEM), a computer program used to assess fatigue and identify problem areas as part of the Service Life Assessment Program (SLAP). This SLAP would show the Viking had considerably more service life available than had originally been estimated.

Overall, the flight tests were highly successful and confirmed the performance and

YS-3A No. 4 (BuNo. 157995), with 60 sonoguoy chutes located to the rear of the underside of its fuselage, approaches USS *Forrestal* (CV-59) during carrier suitability tests in November 1973. There are Aero-1D fuel tanks on the wing stations and the wing trailing edge flaps are deployed. (Robert Lawson Collection)

In 1975 the Navy tests the AGM-84D Harpoon anti-shipping missile on the S-3A platform. The Harpoon was, however, deployed on the P-3C Orion and later the A-6E Intruder and was not mated with the Viking until the Weapons System Improvement Program (WSIP), which became the S-3B. The Viking became the lead carrier-based Harpoon platform, able to utilize all of the Harpoon's features. The Harpoon was later replaced by the AGM-84H/K SLAM/SLAM-ER. (United States Navy via Richard Burgess, USN. [Ret.])

handling qualities Lockheed had predicted. Indeed, the sole modification involved the addition of small metal strips on the leading edge of the wings between the fuselage and the engine pylons to reduce the incidence of stalls.

From an engine perspective, the TF34-GE-2 ran for the first time in April 1969, one month ahead of schedule. However, the program experienced problems beginning in late 1970 as the GE-2, weighing in at 1,421 lbs, could not meet the Navy's 1,260-lb weight specification. The Navy granted a deviation in exchange for a program cost reduction and the final engine weighed 1,478 lbs.

At the same time that GE was testing the -2 turbofan engine, the Navy was conducting its own evaluations at the Naval Air Propulsion Test Center. Altitude tests were performed from February through August 1971. Additional tests were conducted from September 1971 through January 1972, focusing on inlet distortion, anti-ice, rocket gas, climatic, air starts, and altitude performance and transient qualifications.

The first flight of the YTF34 engine occurred on 22 January 1971 at GE's Flight Test Center in California. Production of the -2 was authorized on 3 March 1971.

Flight testing was conducted using an NB-47 Flying Engine Test Bed (53-2104). The engine had been installed in an S-3A nacelle and flown on the wing of the NB-47. The engine was tested for 330 hours through September 1972. Tests revealed a host of problems, ranging from reduced starter assist air-start envelope, reduced windmill air-start capability, altitude compressor stalls, engine rollback with S-3A load, and main fuel control "G" load sensitivity. The TF34-GE-2 engine successfully completed all qualification test requirements on 25 August 1972, although correction of the problems had set the program back some two months.

The first production engine was delivered to Lockheed in August 1972 and the -2 became fleet operational in February 1974. Several problems developed during the initial operation with VS-41 resulting from non-specified engine duty cycle. The Viking, and subsequently its engines, were designed for long-endurance patrol missions, during which the engines were expected to be subjected to fewer throttle transients and to be operated for extended periods of time at idle flight, conditions that were relatively easy on the engine. During flight operations at VS-41, which was charged with training Viking pilots, the aircraft were subjected to numerous take-offs and landings and the rigors of formation flight, all of which necessitated heavy throttle movements. These additional engine cycles and throttle movements led to high-temperature engine problems, resulting in the need to prematurely replace the first-stage turbine nozzle diaphragms. This was resolved by replacing the original impingement-cooled first-stage turbine with a film-cooled leading edge diaphragm.

The -400A also incorporated a modified fuel control and configuration changes, different external piping and an adaptive control system for optimizing accessory power extraction. A subsystem was added to avoid engine stalls when the engine ingested exhaust gases from rockets launched from stations near the engine inlets.

The problems noted during the initial flight operations were corrected by September 1972, resulting in the TF34-GE-400A. The first -400As were delivered in December 1974.

The Viking features the Douglas 1-E Escapac zero-zero ejection seat, which can be jettisoned from a zero-speed, zero-altitude. This image shows the original ejection seat tests conducted on an S-3A mock-up cabin section using a rocket-propelled sled. The seats have a command (crew) and individual eject mode. Under command eject, the two aft crew member seats ejected 0.5 seconds prior to the forward crew members and at slightly different trajectories to maintain time and lateral separation. (Lockheed Martin Company)

A VS-22 *Checkmate* S-3A performs a touch-and-go over the deck of the USS *Saratoga* (CV-60) in January 1980. Modex 700 was assigned to the so-called CAG bird aircraft flown by the Commander, Carrier Air Wing (still called CAG from the days of when they were called Commander, Carrier Air Group) when he flew with the squadron. The CAG aircraft carried the most colorful markings in the squadron. (Robert Lawson Collection)

S-3A

The S-3A Viking ushered in a new era of carrier-based anti-submarine warfare capability. Regardless of the category, the Viking stood superior in comparison to the S-2G. The Viking's performance more than doubled that of the Tracker; the Viking had a maximum speed of 518 m.p.h. (450 knots), a range of over 2,300 miles (3,700km), and could climb to altitudes beyond 35,000 feet (10,668 meters) The S-3A could also cover a search area of over three times that of the Tracker, and could carry more weapons and sonobuoys. These features allowed the Viking to undertake additional new missions, including electronic and sea surface surveillance, communications relay, and search and rescue.

The S-3A featured a high wing configuration, contributing to the aircraft's reputation as one of the most maneuverable aircraft in the fleet. This construction provided the aircraft with lift needed for low speeds and gave the Viking a nearly six-to-one airspeed ratio, with a stall speed of about 80 knots. Another significant feature was the Viking's large vertical tail surface, measuring 22 ft. 9 in. Carrier stowage was accomplished through mechanical wing and tail-fold mechanisms, which folded the wings above the fuselage in a side-by-side fashion, and the tailfin folded down to the left. The Viking took up approximately eight percent more deck space than the Tracker.

Primary flight controls were provided through a system of elevators and a trimmable, adjusted horizontal stabilizer, ailerons augmented by upper and lower surface wing spoilers and a large rudder. Control surfaces were deflected hydraulically. The upper and lower wing spoilers could be activated symmetrically and used as a speed brake. The fuselage consists of a semi-monocoque all-metal fail-safe structure, with two parallel beams forming a keelson from the nose gear to the tail hook and strengthening the overall structure and distributing the force of carrier operations throughout the airframe.

Two General Electric TF34-GE-400-A bypass ratio turbofan engines mounted on wing pylons provided power for the Viking. The engines, which replaced the -2s used in the eight pre-production and early production aircraft, were each rated at 9,275-lbs (41.2 kN) of dry thrust. The same basic engines power the U.S. Air Force A-10 Thunderbolt II, also called the Warthog. The TF34 is a single-stage, front-fan design, with a 14-stage compressor section and two-state high-pressure turbine. Module engine components and split cowls permitted easy access to critical areas for maintenance. An engine change could be accomplished in less than an hour.

Four internal fuel tanks located within the main wing box inboard of the wing-folds held a total of 13,142 lbs (1,933 U.S. gallons). Additional fuel could be carried in wing-mounted drop tanks. An in-flight refueling capability, provided via a centrally located recessed probe just above the windshield, allowed the Viking to stay on station longer.

The S-3's four-person crew consisted of a pilot, a COTAC, who served as co-pilot and assisted with operation of the non-acoustic sensors, a Tactical Coordinator (TACCO), who coordinated all tactical operations during the mission, and a SENSO, who manned the Viking's acoustic sensors. An Aviation Warfare Specialist (AW), the SENSO was the sole enlisted rank aboard a Viking. The pilot was charged with safety of flight and could

An S-3A from VS-38 *Red Griffins* aboard the USS *Enterprise* (CVN-65) takes part in the RIMPAC '78 Exercise in the western Pacific. An EA-6B Prowler from VAQ-134 is just aft of the Viking as are several F-14A Tomcats from VF-1 *Wolfpack*. The Viking appears to be taxiing toward the bow catapults. (United States Navy via Richard Burgess, USN, [Ret.])

A VS-21 S-3A sits on the tarmac at NAS Moffett Field, Florida, in March 1979. The *Fighting Red Tails* were then deployed as part of CVW-15 aboard USS *Kitty Hawk* (CV-63). (United States Navy via Richard Burgess, USN, [Ret.])

also serve as the mission commander, depending on the crew seniority. The COTAC, originally a naval aviation officer, but later a Naval Flight Officer (NFO), had secondary responsibility for safety of flight and also handled communications and navigation. The shift to NFO occurred during the mid-1970s once it was realized that it would be difficult to accumulate and record flight hours and landings with two pilots. Crew escape during emergencies was accomplished by the McDonnell Douglas Escapac 1E zero-zero ejection seat.

At the heart of the S-3A lay the advanced Univac 1832 General Purpose Digital Computer (GPDC), which was derived from the 1831 used in the P-3 Orion, but specially built for the Viking. The 1831, military designation AN/AYK-10, was a smaller and more rugged version of the 1832, designed to withstand the harsher carrier environment and the jolt of carrier launch and landing. The AYK-10 was considered "state-of-the-art" at the time of its inception, and marked the first time a digital computer had been used to integrate an aircraft's sensors and navigation systems. Also representing a significant advance for its time, the AYK-10's software utilized three basic programs to control operations, test procedures, and weapons. The weapons system program contained the various mission databases used by Viking's sensors to compare and classify threats as well as evaluate geographical and oceanographic conditions.

The Viking packed a substantial communications suite that consisted of two AN/ARC-156A Ultra High frequency (UHF) radios for short-range voice and data communications, an AN/ARC-153A High Frequency (HF) radio for long-range communications (clear or encrypted data or clear-voice), a seven-point LS-601/AI inter-plane communications system, an AN/APX-72 Identify Friend or Foe (IFF) receiver/interrogator, a KY-58 cryptographic system for secure voice communications, and an encrypted Link-11 data link. All radios were five-digit capable.

The primary navigation equipment consisted of the AN/ASN-92(V) Carrier Aircraft Inertial Navigation System (CAINS) and the AN/APN-200 Doppler Navigation System. The Viking also has the AN/APN-202 Radar Beacon Transponder, AN/ARN-83 Low Frequency Automatic Directional Finder, and AN/ARN-84 TACAN. Carrier approaches were aided by the AN/ASW-25 Automatic Carrier Landing System (ACLS) and the AN/ARA-63 Instrument Carrier Landing System (ICLS).

Initial deliveries of the S-3A went to Anti-Submarine Air Squadron Forty-One (VS-41), the Anti-Submarine Warfare Fleet Replenishment Squadron (FRS) at NAS North Island, California, which at the time had responsibilities for training all Viking crews. VS-21 was the first operational squadron to receive the new Viking and began its transition from the S-2G in July 1974. Although the Viking went to sea as part of a Detachment with VS-29 aboard USS *John F. Kennedy* (CV-67) in mid-to-late 1975, the aircraft's first full squadron deployment was in 1976 aboard USS *Enterprise* (CVN-65). Conversion continued at a fast pace and by the end of 1977, the transition to the Viking had been completed. VS-37 was the last to transition to the Viking. By 1978, the Navy was operating 11 fleet squadrons consisting of 10 planes each, based at NAS Cecil Field on the East Coast and NAS North Island on the West Coast, and one fleet replenishment squadron based at North Island.

As this Viking banks hard to the left, its left wing's upper surface spoilers Numbers 1 and 2 are actuated. The Viking's high wing helps provide the lift needed for slow speeds and loitering. This S-3A is the Bicentennial Viking from Sea Control Squadron VS-41 *Shamrocks,* **designated to commemorate the 200th anniversary of the United States in 1976. (The Tail Hook Association via Author)**

The main undercarriage consists of three struts and is derived from the undercarriage of the Vought F-8 Crusader. Vought teamed with Lockheed during the VSX proposal stage to bring into the production mix a manufacturer with carrier aviation experience so as to better compete against Grumman, which manufactures the Avenger, Mauler, and the Tracker. Vought had a successful history with the A-7E Corsair II and the F-8 Crusader as well as the F4U Corsair of World War II. (Jose Ramos)

Its wings folded for easier stowage, this S-3A (BuNo. 160160) from VS-38 *Red Griffins,* takes its place aboard USS *Constellation* (CV-64) in 1980 with two Vought A-7 Corsair II light attack bombers in the background. At this point in its career, the S-3A's primary mission was ASW and surface surveillance. (LCDR Richard B. Burgess, USN, [Ret.])

Attached to the bow catapult, an S-3A awaits launch. The Viking's launch bar and nose gear assembly are derived from the A-7 Corsair II. The wrap-around windshield offers a 17° look-down capability. Clearly visible are the two large windshield wipers. The black antenna on the top of the fuselage is for UHF/IFF and the second blade antenna is part of the Sonobuoy Receiver System (SRS). (Robert Lawson Collection)

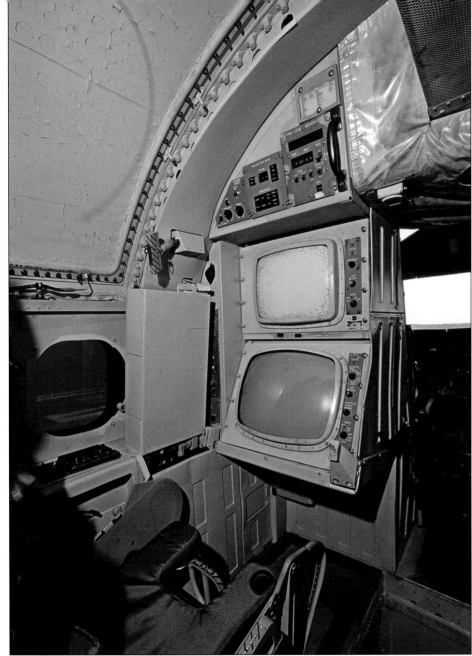

The SENSO station on the S-3A and early S-3B is in the aft left crew station behind the pilot. The SENSO, an aviation warfare specialist (AW), was the sole enlisted person aboard the Viking. The SENSO operated the acoustic processors. This station features a Multi-Purpose Display (MPD) for monitoring non-acoustic sensors and a smaller Auxiliary Read-out Unit (ARU) for monitoring the acoustic sensors. (LCDR Tom Twomey, USN)

The pilot and COTAC stations are clearly visible here. In early Viking crews two naval aviators occupied the front seats. Soon, however, concerns over quantifying flight time and arrested landings led to replacement of the second aviator with a naval flight officer (NFO). (LCDR Tom Twomey, USN)

The crew entry for the Viking is on the right side of the fuselage near the TACCO station. (LCDR Tom Twomey, USN)

A Viking operates on the deck of a carrier in the Persian Gulf in June 2006. In previous years, VS-24 Scouts had operated with CVW-8 aboard USS *Theodore Roosevelt* (CVN-71) during Desert Storm, flying more than 449 combat sorties and logging 990 flight hours. A Scout (BuNo. 159743) attacked and destroyed an Iraqi AAA site on an island near Kuwait City on 2 February 1991, using six Mk 82 iron bombs launched from TERs. VS-24 disestablished on 31 March 2007. (United States Navy)

On carrier approach, the handling of the Viking is very similar to that of the A-6E Intruder, and few mishaps have been recorded. The Viking's approach speed was 100-110 knots (155-126 mph). This aircraft's trailing edge flaps are lowered to the 35° position to improve lift during landing. This S-3A flew with VS-37 *Sawbucks* based at NAS North Island, California. The *Sawbucks'* 1993 cruise marked the first West Coast S-3B deployment. (Robert Lawson Collection)

The TACCOs station is located behind the COTAC. The TACCO is responsible for the overall tactical operations of the aircraft. This station can monitor information from all of the Viking's sensors. The station features a large MPD and an interactive INCOS keyboard and trackball to interface the mission computer and sensors. (LCDR Tom Twomey, USN)

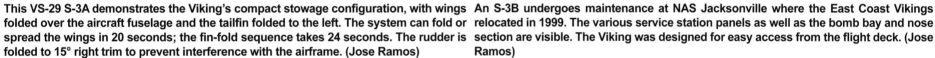

This VS-29 S-3A demonstrates the Viking's compact stowage configuration, with wings folded over the aircraft fuselage and the tailfin folded to the left. The system can fold or spread the wings in 20 seconds; the fin-fold sequence takes 24 seconds. The rudder is folded to 15° right trim to prevent interference with the airframe. (Jose Ramos)

An S-3B undergoes maintenance at NAS Jacksonville where the East Coast Vikings relocated in 1999. The various service station panels as well as the bomb bay and nose section are visible. The Viking was designed for easy access from the flight deck. (Jose Ramos)

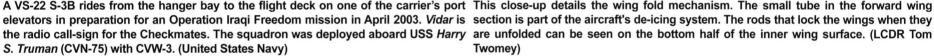

A VS-22 S-3B rides from the hanger bay to the flight deck on one of the carrier's port elevators in preparation for an Operation Iraqi Freedom mission in April 2003. *Vidar* is the radio call-sign for the Checkmates. The squadron was deployed aboard USS *Harry S. Truman* (CVN-75) with CVW-3. (United States Navy)

This close-up details the wing fold mechanism. The small tube in the forward wing section is part of the aircraft's de-icing system. The rods that lock the wings when they are unfolded can be seen on the bottom half of the inner wing surface. (LCDR Tom Twomey)

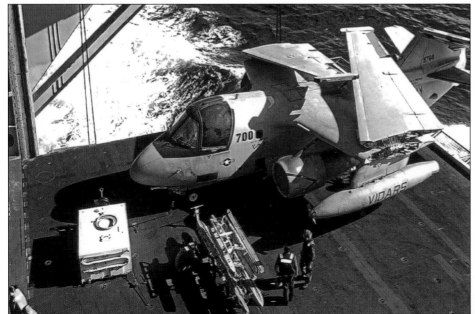

Sporting high-visibility markings, two VS-38 S-3A Vikings refuel over the Sierra Nevada Mountains in about 1989. The lead Viking carries a refueling store and an Aero-1D drop tank, while the trailing Viking appears to be carrying no external stores. The aircraft's refueling probe, located centerline above the cockpit, is extended to meet the refueling aircraft's basket. (United States Navy)

A S-3A armed with iron bombs or mines sits on Catapult No. 1 as its wings unfold prior to launch, in an image that appears to date from the 1970s. (USN)

A head-on view of an S-3B shows the high wing configuration, which was needed for take-off and slow-speed maneuvering. The apparent hole on the elevator is the Ram air intake, which provides air for the cooling system. (CAPT Chris Buhlmann, USNR)

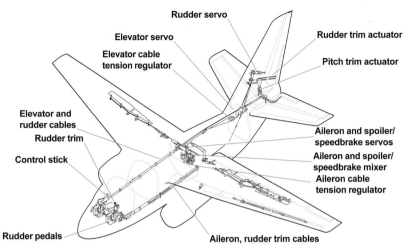

Rudder servo

Elevator servo

Elevator cable
tension regulator

Rudder trim actuator

Pitch trim actuator

Elevator and
rudder cables

Rudder trim

Control stick

Aileron and spoiler/
speedbrake servos

Aileron and spoiler/
speedbrake mixer

Aileron cable
tension regulator

Rudder pedals

Aileron, rudder trim cables

The chance of mechanical failure aboard the Viking is reduced by the fact that the aircraft's flight control systems are powered by two independent hydraulic systems. If either unit became inoperable, the remaining unit could operate all flight control systems. (S-3 NATOPS Manual)

The diagram highlights the significant flight control surfaces of the Viking and Shadow. The flight control system consists of elevators and a trimmable, adjusted horizontal stabilizer, ailerons augments by upper- and lower-surface wing spoilers, and a large rudder. The speed brakes are made up of six panels – two located on each upper wing and one on each lower wing area. The speed brakes are controlled by a thumb switch on the right side of the pilot and COTAC's No. 2 throttle. (S-3 NATOPS Manual)

Loaded with Mk 76 practice bombs on TERs, this aircraft is *en route* to the NAS Fallon target complex in Nevada in January 1986. The Viking *Gamblers* of VS-28 flew out of NAS Cecil Field, Florida, and made their first cruise with the CVW-6 aboard the USS *America* (CV-66) in April 1976. The squadron originally carried the 6XX Modex, but later adopted the 7XX Modex common to VS squadrons. The *Gamblers* flew in Operation Urgent Fury in Grenada in 1983. (LCDR Kurt Garland, USN, [Ret.])

These six S-3A Vikings represent the Atlantic Fleet Viking squadrons. From left to right they are VS-32, VS-31, VS-30, VS-28, VS-24, and VS-22. These Vikings wear the traditional high-visibility markings that were common in the 1960s-1980s. (Robert Lawson Collection)

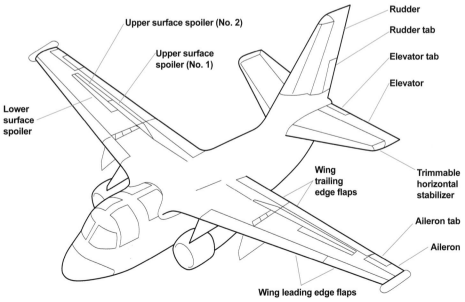

Upper surface spoiler (No. 2)

Upper surface
spoiler (No. 1)

Lower
surface
spoiler

Rudder

Rudder tab

Elevator tab

Elevator

Wing
trailing
edge flaps

Trimmable
horizontal
stabilizer

Aileron tab

Aileron

Wing leading edge flaps

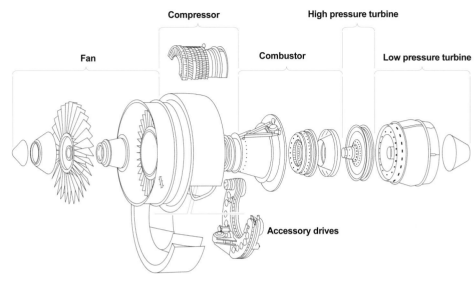

Fan

Compressor

High pressure turbine

Combustor

Low pressure turbine

Accessory drives

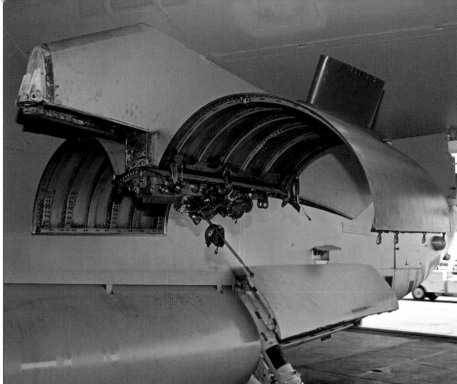

The Viking's power plant is the General Electric TF34-GE-400A turbofan engine. The TF34-GE-400A is a 9,275-lb (41.25kN)-thrust dual-rotor, front-fan engine that features a single-stage fan with a bypass ratio of 6.2, a pressure ratio of 1.5:1, and airflow of 338 lbs per second. The engine has a 14-stage axial-flow compressor on the HP shaft producing a 14:1 pressure ratio and total core airflow of 47 lbs per second. The TF 34 was designed to be a low-risk engine to meet severe reliability requirements in the ASW role within a short time. GE drew upon proven technologies in its TF64, TF39, and GE 1 engines. (S-3 NATOPS Manual)

Flight testing was conducted using an Air Force NB-47 Flying Engine Test Bed (53-2104). The engine had been installed in an S-3A nacelle and flown on the wing of the NB-47. The engine was tested for 330 hours through September 1972. (Kenneth Katz).

The Viking engines are carried in a wing-mounted nacelle, which can be easily opened to facilitate a quick change of the TF34 engine. (Jose Ramos)

An engine pod carries the TF34-GE-400A. The engine control system was designed to minimize the effect of rocket gas ignition from weapons stores. When the trigger is depressed to fire the rocket, the engine ignition is activated and maintained for 5 to 15 seconds. The engine also features separate idle schedules for ground and flight regimes. In flight, the idle schedule varies engine idle speed with altitude. Engine mounts are placed at a slight 9.5° nose-down angle. Because the primary mission of the Viking was to find and destroy submarines, the engines needed to provide both high subsonic flight speed (to reach the target quickly) and long endurance over the target (to locate and prosecute the attack). (LCDR Tom Twomey / USN)

S-3A Sensors

The advances introduced by the Viking were not confined to its remarkable flight performance. The S-3A's overall sensor suite represented a quantum leap in technology over its predecessor and formed the core of the Viking's enhanced mission attributes. The Viking's sensors can be viewed in more than one way: acoustic versus non-acoustic and active versus passive.

Given the S-3A's intended primary mission as an ASW platform, the most significant sensor was its sonar suite. The sonobuoy system consisted of the 31-channel ARR-76 fixed-tuned FM receiver for sonobuoy RF reception, the OL-82A/AYS Acoustic Data Processor System (ADPS), and the ARS-2 Sonobuoy Receiver (SRX). Sonobuoys were released into the water where they would monitor noises that were then transmitted back via VHF frequencies to the Viking over an FM channel where they were received and processed through the acoustic processor. These data were then displayed on the TACCO and/or SENSO's displays. The SRX received sonobuoy signals through a single blade antenna (AS-3675) plus a series of 12-blade aerials (part of the SRS) positioned around the fuselage, which provided 360-degree coverage. The crew could monitor signals from up to 16 sonobuoys and, using dual AN/ASH-27A Analog Tape Recorders (ATR), record up to 16 channels of acoustic data, filtered MAD, sonobuoy commands, and ICS information, which could be stored and reviewed later.

The sonobuoys themselves (officially referred to as search stores) were housed in 60 chutes located on the aft underside of the fuselage behind the bomb bay and arranged in a cross pattern. The buoys were discharged from the chutes using a small explosive charge. Vikings carried a variety of A-sized prepackaged sonobuoys, some "active" like the SSQ-62 Directional Command-Active Sonobuoy System (DICASS) buoy, and others "passive," like the SSQ-41 Low-Frequency Analysis and Recording (LOFAR) buoy, the SSQ-53 Directional Frequency Analysis and Recording (DIFAR) buoy, or the SSQ-77 Vertical Line-Array DIFAR (VLAD) buoy. Other special purpose buoys – for example, the Mk-25 and Mk-58 smoke and a single search and rescue (SAR) buoy – were also carried. The total maximum weight for all buoys was 2,154 lbs.

Buoys were loaded prior to the mission based on anticipated threats. Unlike the chutes on the Orion, the Viking's chutes could only be loaded externally and could not be reloaded in flight. Thus, Viking crews had to pre-plan their sonobuoy loads based upon anticipated threats as determined by regional intelligence.

Additional passive sensors included the Texas Instruments AN/OR-89 Forward-Looking InfraRed (FLIR) unit, a retractable Texas Instruments AN/ASQ-81 Magnetic Anomaly Detector (MAD), and the wingtip-mounted ALR-47 passive ESM. The FLIR

An S-3A from VS-22 flies above the destroyer USS *Adams* (DDG-2). The Viking's FLIR unit is deployed for visual identification. The *Checkmates* were assigned to CVW-3 aboard USS *Saratoga* (CV-60) at this time. From an operator's perspective, the FLIR was often used with the APS-116 radar for target classification. The FLIR provided manual or computer-assisted azimuth coverage of +/- 200° (for a total of 360° coverage) and elevation coverage of 0° to -84°. (Robert Lawson Collection)

Two VS-31 S-3A make their way back to the nuclear powered aircraft carrier USS *Dwight D. Eisenhower* (CVN-69) in mid-1978. Viking 707 (BuNo. 159767) has an empty TER on its right wing station. This photo presents a good view of the wingtip-mounted ALR-47 ESM receivers. The ALR-47 could pin-point and identify radar and electronic emissions to develop an overall electronic order of battle (EOB) or to assist in surface ship classification. (LCDR Richard B. Burgess, USN, [Ret.])

23

was housed in a retractable ventral turret just forward of the aircraft's bomb bay, which provided a full 360 degrees of lateral coverage and permitted elevation coverage of 0° to -84°. The FLIR image was viewed through a 15°-by-20° cone with a 3x telescopic zoom and both auto-focus and auto-track capabilities. FLIR images could then be recorded on a 16mm video camera, using either a one-foot-per-second or 10-feet-per-second speed.

The MAD was another passive sensor, although it was designed more as a confirmation than a detection sensor. The boom extended approximately 19 feet from the aircraft's tail section, and when in operation, permitted Viking crews to fine tune a submarine's location through fluctuations in the earth's magnetic field. The boom was magnetically "clean." The aircraft had a nine-term compensator (the ASA-65) to suppress unwanted magnetic "noise." MAD operations were controlled by the COTAC. The aircraft also had an autopilot function that was engaged prior to MAD operations to compensate the equipment for optimal performance. MAD imagery was displayed in both a raw and interpreted format. Compared to the S-2 MAD, the Viking's ASQ-81 brought nearly twice the range.

The ALR-47 ESM system worked in conjunction with an array of wingtip-mounted sensors that detected radar and electronic emissions, allowing Viking crews to use a line-of-bearing trace to determine the location of enemy radars, SAM, and AAA sites, and other electronic threats. At the time the Viking deployed, the ALR-47 represented the most advanced ESM used by a carrier-based aircraft. The ALR-47 relied on a vast collection of stored threat emitters in the Viking's computer. Information collected by the ESM could be recorded and analyzed at a later time. Over the years, Viking crews discovered that their own experience in analyzing ESM signals was often superior to the computer libraries.

The Viking's active sensor was the Texas Instruments AN/APS-116 high-resolution search radar. The first ASW radar designed specifically to detect periscope-sized targets in high sea states, the APS-116 can search up to 150 nautical miles (in Mode III long-range search-and-navigation mode) over a 240-degree forward arch. The APS-116 was an I-band radar with three operational modes: Mode I – periscope; Mode II – maritime surveillance; and Mode III – long-range search and navigation. Mode I used fast scan (300 rpm), high PRF (2,000 pps), and higher resolution, and had a range selectable up to 32 nm (28 miles). Mode II offered similar range, but used low PRF and slow scan (6 rpm). Mode III offered the greatest range and combined high resolution, low PRF (500 pps), and medium scan (40 rpm). While the COTAC, TACCO, and SENSO could monitor scan-converted information in either Plan Position indicator (PPI) or B-scan format on their displays, only the TACCO and SENSO could process raw radar. One of the unique features of the APS-116 allowed the operator to store images from a single radar sweep to be reviewed later, or to select targets while not emitting.

Crews would often use the APS-116 radar in conjunction with the Viking's FLIR. Operators would use the radar to locate and classify targets and then perform a radar-to-FLIR hand-off to continue monitoring the target passively. The APS-116 represented a significant leap in capability over the APS-88 radar used by the Tracker, which was a weather radar.

A VS-41 S-3A practices off the coast of San Diego in September 1974, its flaps positioned in the loiter position. The ASQ-81(V) MAD allowed Viking crews to pinpoint submerged enemy submarines by differentiating the vessel hull's magnetic signature from the Earth's ambient magnetic field. A digital MAD, the ASQ-208, was tested during the 1990s; despite its three-fold increase in performance, it was not adopted. (Robert Lawson Collection)

This close-up shows the MAD boom extended for maintenance. In flight, the boom is controlled by the COTAC; the boom will not extend when there is weight on the wheels. Ground extension is accomplished by a double-redundant switch located it the service compartments. The boom extends 18 feet from the aircraft and is magnetically clean. The AN/ASA-65 compensator group suppresses any extraneous magnetic noise generated by the aircraft or the environment. (LCDR Tom Twomey, USN)

This Viking FLIR is extended for observation. The S-3A is from VS-28, which was deployed aboard USS *Forrestal* (CV-59) in 1990. The aircraft's fin displays low-visibility "deck of cards" denoting the squadron's moniker, *Gamblers*. The remainder of the aircraft is painted with low-visibility two-tone markings. (Tail Hook Association via Author)

This photo affords a detailed image of the S-3B FLIR – the OR-263. A majority of the FLIR upgrade modifications addressed its reliability rather than enhance its capabilities over the OR-89/A. (LCDR Tom Twomey, USN)

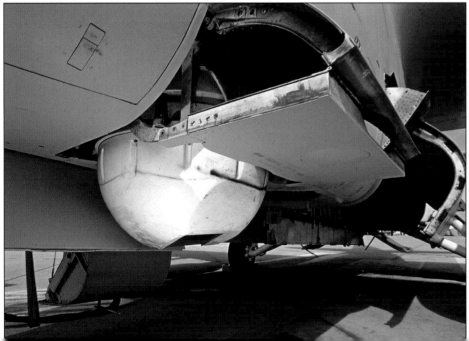

The AS3637 antenna, shown here, is a conventional parabolic dish located in the nose radome. The antenna radiates and receives RF energy for radar and IFF operations. The Texas Instruments AN/APS-116 was the original Viking radar. It was upgraded to the APS-137(V) standard as part of the S-3B Weapons Systems Improvement Program (WSIP) begun in 1981. The APS-137 introduced a fourth operational mode – imaging – which significantly enhanced the Viking's long-range identification capability. (Jose Ramos)

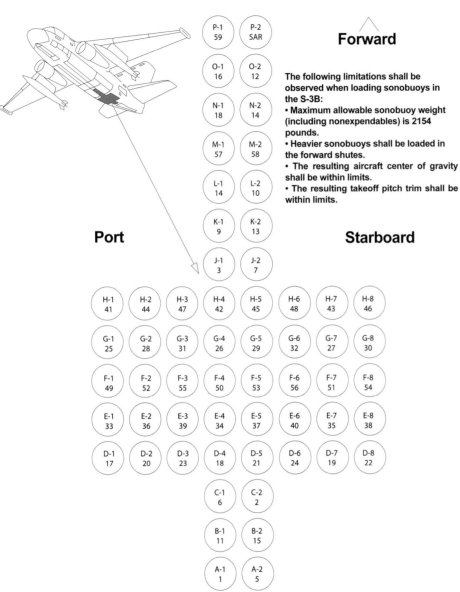

P-1 59	P-2 SAR
O-1 16	O-2 12
N-1 18	N-2 14
M-1 57	M-2 58
L-1 14	L-2 10
K-1 9	K-2 13
J-1 3	J-2 7

Forward

The following limitations shall be observed when loading sonobuoys in the S-3B:
• Maximum allowable sonobuoy weight (including nonexpendables) is 2154 pounds.
• Heavier sonobuoys shall be loaded in the forward shutes.
• The resulting aircraft center of gravity shall be within limits.
• The resulting takeoff pitch trim shall be within limits.

Port

Starboard

H-1 41	H-2 44	H-3 47	H-4 42	H-5 45	H-6 48	H-7 43	H-8 46
G-1 25	G-2 28	G-3 31	G-4 26	G-5 29	G-6 32	G-7 27	G-8 30
F-1 49	F-2 52	F-3 55	F-4 50	F-5 53	F-6 56	F-7 51	F-8 54
E-1 33	E-2 36	E-3 39	E-4 34	E-5 37	E-6 40	E-7 35	E-8 38
D-1 17	D-2 20	D-3 23	D-4 18	D-5 21	D-6 24	D-7 19	D-8 22

C-1 6	C-2 2
B-1 11	B-2 15
A-1 1	A-2 5

Numerals on the image of each of the sonobuoy chutes indicate the buoy jettison sequence. Buoy mix was determined before launch based on the anticipated threat and ocean geography, but was subject to a 2,154-lb. maximum weight. The loading process consisted of manually inserting each buoy into the chute, pushing it until it contacted the breach, and then twisting it a quarter-turn to lock it into place. (S-3 NATOPS Manual)

The sonobuoy chutes are arranged in a cross pattern on the aircraft's underbelly. A total of 60 chutes, one for a dedicated SAR buoy, can carry a variety of Class A-sized active and passive buoys. Data received from the sonobuoys can be analyzed at the SENSO and TACCO stations. The acoustic data processing system (ADPS) can process and monitor active and passive sonobuoys simultaneously. (LCDR Tom Twomey, USN)

Two VS-33 *Screwbird* Vikings are shown with MAD booms extended. These S-3As carry markings from the squadron's 1970-80 scheme, most notably the large "Viking" sword. The markings from the 1990s forward can be seen on page 31. (The Tail Hook Association)

A VS-28 S-3A in ASW prosecution prepares for a simulated attack on a submarine. The MAD boom is extended and a Mk 46 NEARTIP lightweight torpedo is visible in the left bay. (Robert Lawson Collection)

An S-3A, belonging to VS-21 *Fighting Red Tails,* prepares to catch a three-wire aboard USS *John F. Kennedy* (CV-67). The landing gears are rather lazily extended to accommodate the impact of the carrier landing. (Robert Lawson Collection)

A front quarter angle view provides an excellent view of an S-3B in-flight. From VS-38, this Viking carriers an Aero-1D drop tank on its right wing station and a buddy-store on its left wing station. Although wearing a CAG-bird 700 Modex, this Viking has the names of the Deputy CAG affixed on its cockpit station. (Sea Control Wing Atlantic via Author)

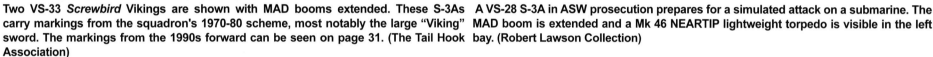

S-3B

While the S-3A was certainly a leap in technology and performance, the Viking of the late 1970s and early 1980s found itself facing the same dilemma as had faced the Tracker in the early 1960s – Soviet submarines were continuing to improve. Moreover, it was equally becoming apparent that the Viking had its own shortcomings, such as a limited ability to place and monitor sonobuoys, the inability to classify targets at long range, the complete lack of a long-range anti-surface weapon, and an inability to defend itself from missile attack. Indeed, the last three of these deficiencies meant that the Viking had a limited role in any power projection mission where enemy air defenses were present.

The solution to these problems came in the Weapons System Improvement Program (WSIP). Begun in 1981, the WSIP sought to convert 160 S-3A Vikings into an improved variant, designated the S-3B, which could operate in the current and anticipated threat environments of the 1980s. As part of this program, Lockheed modified two S-3As (BuNos. 159742 and 160591) to S-3B (also called Bravo) standards.

The first demonstrator Bravo flew on 13 September 1984. The S-3B underwent Operational Evaluation beginning the following March. Although 160 of the improved variant were originally planned, only 119 S-3As were converted to the new Bravo standard. The bulk of the conversions took place at NAS Cecil Field, Florida. The first S-3B was delivered to VS-27, the East Coast S-3B Fleet Replenishment Squadron, in December 1987, and the first fleet delivery took place in July 1988 to VS-30's *Diamondcutters*. East Coast squadrons completed the transition to the S-3B in July 1991; conversions from the S-3A on the West Coast began in March 1992 and were completed in September 1994. A combined detachment from VX-1 and VS-27 made the Bravo's first carrier deployment in 1988 aboard USS *Forrestal* as part of the Teamwork '88 Exercise in the North Atlantic. VS-31 *Topcats,* however, made the S-3B's first full squadron deployment in 1990. The last S-3A squadron (VS-38) completed its transition to the Bravo in 1994.

The majority of changes associated with the S-3B (effectuated through Air Frame Change (AFC) -208/Engineering Change Proposal (ECP) No. S3-400) involved the aircraft's sensors. Most significant was the addition of the APS-137(V)(1) radar, which introduced Inverse Synthetic Aperture Radar (ISAR) processing. Accessible via Mode IV, ISAR allowed operators to identify targets, typically ships, from well outside the threat envelope and permitted classification of enemy ships by type and size. Rather than displaying a non-descript "blip," which told operators only that something was present, the ISAR used the target's motion to create a moving Doppler referenced image

The S-3B demonstrator (BuNo. 159742) makes its maiden flight carrying two simulated AGM-84D Harpoon anti-ship missiles. Conceived in 1965 as a replacement for the AGM-12 Bullpup, the Harpoon Block 1C (Charlie) carried by the Viking packed a 488.5-lb high-explosive (HE) penetration warhead and had a top speed in excess of Mach 0.85. The Viking was the lead air wing Harpoon asset due to its superb targeting capabilities. (Robert Lawson Collection)

The S-3B began test flights from the Lockheed facilities in Palmdale, California, on 13 September 1984. The Bravo, as it was sometimes called, introduced improved avionics and weapons systems, including a new acoustic processor and sonobuoy receiver, an improved computer, ISAR radar capability, and electronic countermeasures. The ALE-39 expendables dispenser appears just below the "Navy" marking as a large black box. (United States Navy via LCDR Richard B. Burgess, USN, [Ret.])

or blob. That moving image could then be frozen to visualize and identify the target ship – operators called this process "blobology." Operators could decipher significant features such as masts and superstructure, which allowed classification by ship class. The ISAR ship categorization scheme divided contacts into four basic types – combatants, carriers, small craft, and merchant/auxiliaries. Identification came through a recognition process, moving from the Perception Level, to Gross, and Fine Levels. Thus, a *Knox*-class frigate would be identified as a combatant at the Perceptual Level; a frigate at the Gross Level; and a *Knox*-class frigate, perhaps even by ship name, at the Fine Level. Each classification level required that the target be correctly identified at the previous Level.

The ISAR represented a vast improvement over the S-3A, which had needed to fly into visual range of the target to positively identify it, a procedure that placed the Viking crew directly in harm's way. Despite the advances in technology, there is still nothing that beats a visual identification from a trained and well-prepared crew, and visual identifications were often required by commanding officers.

The S-3B featured a significantly improved ESM suite, the IBM ALR-76, which provided greater frequency coverage and improved bearing accuracy within 2°. The new ESM also gave Viking crews a basic missile threat warning, providing C-band through J-band coverage of both pulsed-and continuous-wave emissions. The ALR-76 used in conjunction with the APS-137 ISAR to provide exceptional target classification from well over 150 miles without over-flying it and, if necessary, to attack that platform from outside the Viking's maximum engagement range. According to Viking aircrews, the combination of the ISAR with the ALR-76 ESM yielded about as positive an identification as one could get.

Closely associated with the ALR-76 was the fleet standard Marconi ALE-39 chaff/flare dispenser. Installed in three 30-unit banks, the dispensers could be used to defeat both infrared and radar-guided missiles. Each unit contained 30 dispensers, which carried a combination of flares, chaff, or radio frequency (RF) jammers and could be released automatically or manually by the pilot, COTAC, or TACCO in a variety of sequences based on timing or the number of units desired. Chaff rounds were pre-cut to varying frequency levels to provide a full-spectrum protection against threat radars. One dispenser was located on each fuselage and the third was located on the aircraft's belly just ahead of the sonobuoy chute. The addition of the ALE-39 meant that the Viking now had a base level self-defense capability, which allowed it to enter higher threat areas of operation.

The S-3B's sonar capabilities were greatly enhanced by replacing the OL-82A Acoustic Data Processor with the IBM UYS-1 Proteus Spectrum Analyzer Unit (SAU) used by the P-3C Update III Orion. Also added was a 99-channel sonobuoy receiver (the Hazeltine Hazeltine ARR-78), which permitted greater buoy monitoring, and a more accurate Sonobuoy Reference System, the ARS-4, and the improved AQH-7(V)2 Analog Tape Recorder. The computer was also upgraded to AYK-10B standards.

The S-3B WSIP also upgraded the FLIR to the new Texas Instruments OR-263, replaced one of the S-3As two MU-576/AYS Drum Memory Systems with the OL-320/AYS Data Processing Group, and although not part of the WSIP, an improved auxiliary power unit (APU). Overall, the WSIP modifications added a mere 601 lbs to the Viking,

changing its characteristics only slightly and maintaining the aircraft's center of gravity within existing limits. Power consumption for the new equipment increased less than 1 KW.

From a weapons perspective, the S-3B was equipped to fire the long-range Boeing AGM-84 Harpoon anti-shipping missile. While the Navy experimented with the Harpoon for the S-3A in 1975, efforts to deploy the missile were shelved in favor of deployment on the Intruder and Orion. With WSIP, the S-3B was then only carrier-based aircraft able to utilize the Harpoon's full capabilities. The Viking's Harpoon capabilities were so significant that the aircraft became the air wing lead for ASUW.

During the late 1990s, and after experiences during the 1991 Gulf War, a limited number of Vikings were also equipped with the imaging infrared AGM-65F Maverick, which provided a lower yield and better-controlled weapon for use in the littoral regions. Beginning in 1996, four S-3Bs were modified to carry two Maverick weapons, and rotated through several fleet squadrons. VS-22 was the first squadron to deploy with the Maverick Vikings in early 1997. The Checkmates kept at least one Maverick-capable Viking airborne during all carrier operations and every SUW alert was manned by a Maverick S-3B. Although one of the Maverick Vikings was lost on March 1998, another Viking (BuNo. 159741) was modified and deployed with VS-30 on its next cruise. Four more Vikings were subsequently modified to meet the growing demand for a Maverick capability.

Two VS-32 *Maulers* fly in formation off the coast of Jacksonville, Florida. Modex 700 (BuNo. 160600) displays the carrier air wing's high-visibility markings of the CAG-bird, while Mauler 701 in the background features a combination of the standard squadron markings of a low-visibility fuselage and a high-visibility tailfin marking. The 701 Modex was typically emblazoned with the Commanding Officer's name. VS-32 was the first S-3B squadron to launch the Harpoon and the first squadron to score a combat kill. (Jose Ramos)

S-3A Viking VS-21 Fighting Redtails

VS-21 was the first fleet squadron to receive the S-3A Viking. Shown here is Modex AB/607 (BuNo. 159407) aboard USS *John F. Kennedy* (CVA-67) with CVW-1 in January 1975. The *Fighting Redtails* transitioned from the S-2E Tracker on 1 July 1974 and were declared operational the following November. VS-21 transitioned to the S-3B in April 1990 was disestablished on 28 August 2005, after having made over 20 deployments with the Viking.

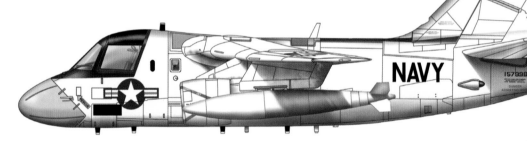

US-3A COD VRC-50 Foo Dogs

One of the first variants proposed, the US-3A was meant to replace the aging C-1 Trader. Lockheed converted YS-3A No. 7 (BuNo. 157998) to a US-3A configuration, removing all of the aircraft's sensors, ASW, and ESM gear, and several antennas, increasing the overall carriage capacity. With two cargo pods, the US-3A could carry 7,400 lbs (3,357 kg) of cargo some 1,920 n.m. (2,208 miles) This US-3A was assigned to VRC-50, the *Foo Dogs,* and served U.S. carriers operating in the Western Pacific.

S-3A Viking "1776" markings

Viking maintainers at North Island's VS-41 celebrated the nation's 200th birthday by painting *Shamrock* 160120 in red, white, and blue bicentennial markings. A large "76" emblem appears on the side fuselage just below the cockpit and the famous saying, "Don't Tread on Me," appeared on the aircraft's tailfin.

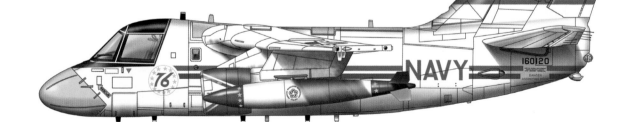

S-3B Viking Prototype

Stemming from the Weapons System Improvement Program (WSIP) begun in 1981, the S-3B emerged as the premier carrier-based anti-submarine platform. Two Vikings (BuNos. 159742 and 160591) were selected to serve as prototypes for the Bravo, with the former, shown here in its test markings, making its first flight on 13 September 1984. 119 S-3As were converted to the Bravo standard, with deliveries starting in December 1987.

ES-3A Shadow, VQ-5 *Sea Shadows*

The *Sea Shadows* of VQ-5 operated the electronic reconnaissance/warfare variant ES-3A Shadow. This Shadow (BuNo. 159405) is from VQ-5's Det D assigned at the time to USS *Kitty Hawk* (CVA-63). The *Sea Shadows* were based at NAS North Island, California.

S-3B Viking VS-24 *Scouts*

The *Scouts* of VS-24 transitioned to the S-3B in September 1989 and was one of the six Viking squadrons participating in Operation Desert Storm in 1991. The *Scouts* flew 449 combat sorties and logged over 990 flight hours while flying with CVW-8 aboard USS *Theodore Roosevelt* (CVN-71). Shown here is the *Scouts* CAG-bird (BuNo. 159743) as it appeared in 1997 on its Mediterranean/Persian Gulf cruise, where it flew missions in support of UN operations in Bosnia and the Iraqi "No-Fly" Zone.

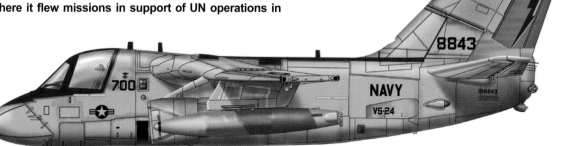

S-3B Viking VS-22 *Checkmates*

VS-22's *Checkmates* were the final S-3 squadron to disestablish on 29 January 2009. The Checkmates transitioned from the S-2E to the S-3A in 1975, and in 1976 were the first Viking squadron to deploy with the aircraft. The *Checkmates* were the first Viking unit to deploy with female aviators. The squadron made the final Viking deployment in 2008, basing out of al-Asad Air Base in Iraq's al-Anbâr Province.

S-3A VS-28 *Gamblers*

The *Gamblers* were based at NAS Cecil Field, Florida, and flew in support of air operations during the 1983 invasion of Grenada, code-named Urgent Fury. VS-28 also flew in support of Navy carrier operations during the Iranian Hostage Crisis. The squadron made its final cruise aboard USS *Forrestal* (CV-59) with CVW-6 in 1991.

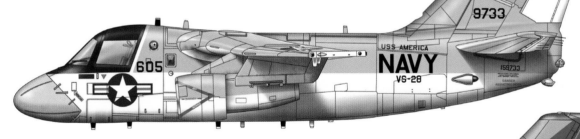

S-3A VS-33 *Screwbirds*
AE/705 BuNo. 160131

This VS-33 *Screwbird* shows off its late 1970s markings. During the 1970s and 1980s, the squadron wore a large sword on the tail fin. This was replaced in the 1990s by a large bird standing with a screw in its stomach.

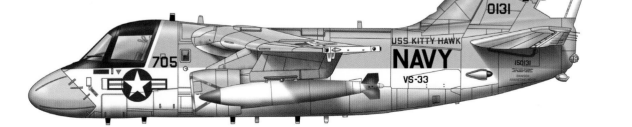

YS-3A No. 5

The fifth pre-production aircraft, BuNo. 157996 was assigned to hydraulic, fuel, air conditioning, and avionics evaluations, and was later modified to be the KS-3A tanker demonstrator. After operating with VS-41 during the early 1980s, the KS-3A was modified to US-3A standards. It served with VRC-50 until 20 January 1989, when it stalled on approach and crashed in the water off Cubi Point. This image shows No. 5 in Lockheed Martin factory markings in early 1974.

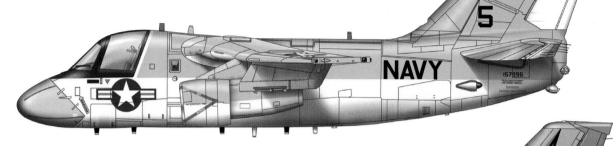

Naval Air Test Center "ASW 9770"

The Navy experimented with several modifications to the Viking, including the test of an ALQ-99 jamming pod. The pod is carried by the EA-6B Prowler, the Navy's electronic warfare/electronic attack aircraft.

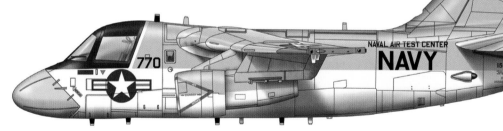

S-3B Outlaw Viking VS-37 *Sawbucks*

VS-37 was one of the few squadrons to operate the experimental "proof-of-concept" demonstrator Outlaw Viking, which offered real-time Over-the-Horizon Targeting capabilities through a combination of GPS and satellite communications (known as OASIS III). The Outlaw Viking concept originated with the P-3C Orion community's Outlaw Hunter program, which had much success during the Gulf War. A single demonstrator aircraft (BuNo. 160124) was modified by Tiburon Systems and can be distinguished by the black SATCOM antenna located on the Viking's top fuselage.

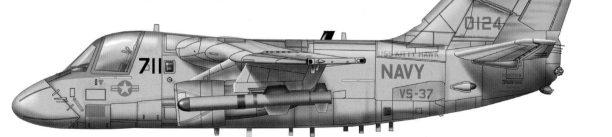

A significant part of the WSIP included the addition of a self-defense capability. The S-3B introduced the ALE-39, which could launch flares, chaff, or RF jammer payloads. Here a sequential release shows the dispersal of flares. The system can be operated by the pilot, COTAC, or TACCO. (CAPT Chris Buhlmann, USNR)

A close-up image of one of the ALE-39 counter-measures banks shows their general arrangement. (LCDR Tom Twomey, USN)

This diagram represents the dispenser housing and expendable module of the ALE-39 system. (S-3 NATOPS Manual)

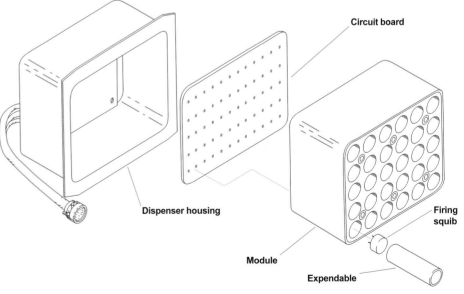

Circuit board

Dispenser housing

Firing squib

Module

Expendable

An S-3B from the Atlantic FRS, VS-27, carries a pair of CATM-84D Harpoons on a training mission. The *Seawolfs* were based at NAS Cecil Field, Florida, and wore the tail code AD, which corresponds to the training squadrons. VS-27 disestablished in September 1994. It trained initial S-3B crews and the first Shadow crews. A Viking from VS-27 performed the last arrested landing and carrier catapult launch from the USS *Saratoga* (CV-60) on 23 June 1994. The Viking was flown by Captain Mark Kitka, who later became the Sea Control Wing Atlantic Commodore. (The Robert Lawson Collection)

An S-3B from VS-41 prepares to launch from one of the bow catapults aboard USS *John Stennis* (CVN-74). (United States Navy)

The AGM-65 Maverick missile was introduced to the Viking in the mid-1990s following the experiences of the 1991 Gulf War. The Maverick proved an effective weapon against surface vessels as well as ground targets. With a LAU-119 launch rail affixed to the wing stations, the aircraft could carry two Mavericks, one on each wing station. Maverick-capable Vikings were in high demand and often sat on Alert 15 status to respond to developing surface threats. (United States Navy)

This VS-33 Viking prepares to tank another aircraft from its 31-301 aerial refueling store (ARS). The ARS permits the Viking to pass fuel at the rate of 1,200 lbs (544kg) per minute. The ARS was carried on the left wing station (W5). (Sea Control Wing Atlantic)

Two colorful S-3B Vikings from VS-21 fly off the coast of Japan. Shown here are Modex 700 and 710. At the time the squadron operated from USS *Kitty Hawk* (CV 63). VS-21 was based at NAF Atsugi, Japan, when the squadron was not deployed aboard *Kitty Hawk*. Following the shift to low-visibility markings that took place in the late 1980s, only the CAG-aircraft (700) and the squadron commander's aircraft (701) wore any significant colors. (Ted Carlson, Fotodynamics).

This close up view of the canopy section of this VS-41 *Shamrock* Viking shows the markings for the Commanding Officer, Commander G. M. Wilson. The Viking provides excellent visibility for both the pilot and COTAC. The Viking, unlike the ES-3A Shadow, can be piloted from both of the front cockpit seats. (Michael N. Tialemasunu, U.S. Navy).

Two Mk 36 Destructor series shallow water mines hang in the right weapons bay. The Destructor series mines were created by adding a Mk 75 Destructor modification kit to existing Mk 80s series iron bombs. The Mk 36 Destructor correlated to a Mk 80 500-lb bomb; Mk 40 correlated to the 1,000-lb Mk 83 bomb, and Mk 41 was the 2,000-lb Mk 84 bomb equivalent. Destructors were discontinued after the Vietnam War when Paris Peace Accord mandated disclosure of how to disarm them to facilitate minefield clearance. The Mk 62 Quickstrike series replaced the Destructors. (Author)

The S-3B received a considerable upgrade to its ESM suite with the replacement of the ALR-47. The ALR-76 offered increased frequency coverage, improved bearing accuracy, and a basic threat warning capability and provided C- through J-Band coverage of both pulsed and continuous wave emissions with a two-degree accuracy. (U.S. Navy)

Viking Weapons

The Viking has two bomb bays, one on each side of the aircraft. Each bomb bay contains two BRU-14/A bomb racks (rated at 850 lbs), which can be configured independently in any of three configurations – parallel, tandem, or special weapons. For example, one bay could carry two torpedoes in tandem while the second carried a single special weapon. The bay stations were designated B1, B2, B3, and B4. The bay doors could be opened or closed in six seconds.

Wing stations could be configured for either single or three weapons, designated as W5 (left wing) and W6 (right wing). Each wing station contained one BRU-11/A bomb rack rated at 2,500 lbs. Triple Ejection Racks (TER) could be carried on one or both wing pylons, giving the capability to carry up to three weapons on each station. Using the TER, Vikings can carry up to six Mk 82 bombs, six Mk-7 dispensers, or six Mk 36 or Mk 40 Destructor mines. TERs can also be configured to carry up to four of the heavier Mk 83 bombs.

The Viking's weapons were initially centered on the aircraft's ASW mission. Although the aircraft carried a variety of depth bombs and mines (moored, CAPTOR, or destructor series), its primary weapon against submarines was the Aerojet Mk 46 lightweight torpedo. The Mk 46 entered service in 1965, but has been improved to the current Mk 46 Mod 5 standard, which incorporated NEARTIP (Near-Term Improvement Program) technology. The Mk 46 carried a 98-lb bulk charge warhead of PBXN-103 high explosives and had a speed of about 46 mph (40 knots) and the ability to re-acquire if its first attack was not successful. The Mk 46 Mod 5A and 5A(S) incorporated improvements to enhance operations in shallow waters.

The Viking could also carry the Mk 50 Barracuda torpedo, developed for use against fast, deep-diving nuclear submarines. The Barracuda used a shaped-charge warhead and was notably faster than the Mk 46, but also cost more. The Barracuda was never cleared for carrier use.

Mines were also a significant part of the Viking offensive capability. Viking's carried a variety of mines for specific purposes, such as moored (the Mk 55 and 56) or CAPTOR mines (the Mk 60). The S-3 could also carry the Mk 53 (325-lb) and -54 (350-lb) depth bomb, which was essentially a depth charge modified for deployment from an aircraft. Another mine resulted from a modification to the standard Mk 80 series iron bomb. Using modification kits, the various Mk 80 bombs could be quickly converted into Destructor or Quickstrike mines. The Mk 36, -40, and -41 Destructor weapons correlated to the

An S-3B from Naval Air Test Center at NAS Patuxent River, Maryland, launches a Mk 50 Barracuda lightweight torpedo. The Mk 50 was developed to specifically counter quieter and deeper-diving Soviet Project 705 *Lira* (NATO designation "Alpha")-class attack submarines, but proved too expensive and was abandoned. The Mk 50 costs approximately $1.14 million per copy, versus the $180,000 per copy of the Mk 46. (Robert Lawson Collection)

Two ordnance men work with an AGM-84E SLAM. The SLAM-ER shares many physical attributes of its Harpoon brethren, but is slightly longer. SLAM-ER reached IOC in June 2000. The missile uses military-grade GPS and infrared navigation and is extremely accurate. Although capable of "fire-and-forget" targeting, it can also be targeted in a "man-in-the-loop" mode. Each SLAM-ER costs approximately $600,000. (PHAN Jessica Davis, U.S. Navy).

Mk 82 (500 lb), Mk 83 (1,000 lb), and Mk 84 (2,000 lb) bombs, with Mk 62 (500-lb) and -65 (2,000-lb) the corresponding Quickstrike designations. The Mk 36 and -40 Destructor mines were capable of retarded (using a Mk15 kit) or free-fall delivery. The Mk 62 Quickstrike was a kit-modified Mk 82 bomb similar to the Mk 36; however, the Mk 65 was a completely redesigned mine utilizing the Mk 65 casing versus a general purpose bomb and an algorithm-driven Target Detection Device.

For anti-surface missions against ships or surface targets, the S-3s could be armed with Mk 82, -83, or -84 general-purpose iron bombs, Mk 7 dispensers for cluster munitions, and LAU-10 (four five-inch rockets), LAU-68 (seven 2.75-inch rockets), and -69 (nineteen 2.75-inch rockets) rocket pods. The Mk 7 dispenser could be loaded with CBU-59 anti-armor, APAM, or Rockeye II submunitions. Special weapons (code name for the B57 nuclear weapon) were also in the Viking arsenal.

The S-3B introduced a significant improvement in the Viking's anti-surface weaponry arsenal with addition of the long-range AGM-84D Harpoon anti-surface missile. The Harpoon meant the Viking could now provide a significant offensive punch against surface targets. Given its APS-137 ISAR, the aircraft proved a superior weapons platform for the missile. The ISAR was significant for target identification and classification which were critical to setting up the attack, but the S-3B Harpoon suite had many more advantages over the other shooters. S-3B crews could select terminal functions such as seeker search priority and search pattern size. These options, combined with waypoints, enable and destruction points, allowed more discrimination in target acquisition.

Concern that the Harpoon, with its 488-lb high-explosive warhead, packed too much punch for smaller shipping and that it targeted too indiscriminately lead to the addition of the AGM-65E laser-guided Maverick and the AGM-65F imaging infrared Maverick for littoral use. The first combat firing of a Maverick took place in March 2003 during Operation Iraqi Freedom. The Maverick offered a weapon system that reduced the risk of targeting the wrong vessel. The Harpoon, for all of its advantages, could acquire a new target, which meant that attacks against ships in multiple ship formations or in the vicinity of friendly vessels presented a risk. The Maverick missile could be carried on either weapon station using a LAU-117(V)2/A rail.

In the late 1990s, a limited number of Viking's were also given the capability to fire and control AGM-84E SLAM and AGM-84H/K SLAM-ER missiles for use against land-based and sea targets, which later developed into the Viking Maverick Plus System (MPS) modification. The SLAM combined the airframe, engine, and warhead of the anti-ship Harpoon with the WGU-10/B IIR seeker of the AGM-65D Maverick and the data link of the AGM-62 Walleye, providing "man-in-the-loop" control. The S-3B carried a single AWW-13 data link pod on wing station W6, which controlled the SLAM after launch, regardless of which aircraft launched the missile. The pod also permitted the Viking to control missiles launched by other platforms.

The combination of Maverick/Harpoon/SLAM capability gave the Viking considerably flexibility in the Surface Search and Classification (SSC) role, allowing it to engage land- and sea-based targets of opportunity.

The S-3B was also modified to carry the ADM-141 Tactical Air Launched Decoy

Each of the bomb bays can be configured to carry one or two weapons. The two BRU-14/A bomb racks, shown here, can be configured independently in any of three configurations – parallel, tandem, or special weapons. For example, one bay could carry two torpedoes in tandem while the second carried a single special weapon. The BRU-14/A provides a 14-in. suspension for weapons weighing up to 1,000 lbs. (Author)

Weapons loads were designated differently depending on the types of weapons carried. This illustration shows the possible designations and release sequences. Special weapons, the code name for nuclear weapons, could be individually released. If stations were released simultaneously, one weapon would be dropped in the normal release sequence, followed by the second. (S-3B Viking NATOPS Manual)

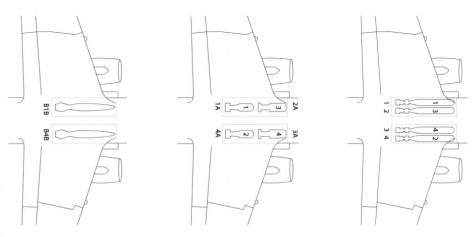

(TALD), which were successfully used during the opening phase of the 1991 Gulf War and later in Bosnia. The TALD was a "glide or stand-off decoy" designed to fool an enemy's air defense system by appearing to be a strike aircraft on enemy air search radars. Once radar operators locked on to the TALD and revealed their position, accompanying strike aircraft launched High-speed Anti-Radar Missile (HARM) to destroy the radar site. The TALD was capable of autonomous flight control using a pre-programmed flight profile executed by an onboard computer. Although the S-3B could carry four TALDs, only two were typically carried, because the fins interfered with one another.

Over the years, the Vikings' missions have included its staple ASW mission (now called Under-Sea Warfare or USW), as well as serving as the air wing's primary Surface Warfare (SUW), Mine Warfare (MIW), Electronic Surveillance (ES), and Armed Surface Reconnaissance (ASR) aircraft. Vikings also fly Counter-Targeting (CTTG), Combat Search and Rescue (CSAR), and Surface Search and Classification (SSC) missions. While Vikings have long been able to perform aerial refueling (tanking) missions, this role became crucial in the late 1990s following the retirement of the A-6 and KA-6D Intruders. Vikings filled the role vacated by the Intruders and served as the sole carrier-based tanking asset until the introduction of the Super Hornet, which performed both mission and overhead tanking.

Most Viking flights involved performing a combination of several missions, including ASW, ESM, SSC and tanking, which are reflected in the mixed weapons loads (called "swing loads") often seen on S-3Bs. Typical ARS swing-loads consisted of a buddy store, a Harpoon/Maverick, two Mk 82s in the bomb bay, and chaff, flare, and ALQ-190 AIr-launched Rapid-Blooming Off-board Chaff (AIRBOC), and allowed Vikings to quickly respond to emerging threats without the carrier having to launch another aircraft. If a submarine threat was present, the Mk 82s in the bomb bay could be replaced with Mk 46 torpedoes or Mk 53 depth bombs.

As the Viking moved away from ASW duties and concentrated more on surface missions, the mining and ASW missions were removed from the Sea Control mission and Viking's weapons loads concentrated on air-to-ground weapons. During the missions in the 2000-2004 time frames, Vikings flew a large number of tanking sorties, which mean that all S-3Bs launched with buddy stores and, in many cases, an auxiliary fuel tank, on the wing stations, and carried Mk 80 series iron bombs in their bomb bays. In instances where surface contacts were anticipated, Mavericks were carried on the right wing (W6), with buddy stores on W5. Maverick-armed Vikings also sat Alert 15, as did Vikings armed with Harpoons, depending on the threat and theater. Vikings also carried SLAM and SLAM-ER missiles and the AWW-13 controller.

As the Viking's career came to an end, missions expanded to include Non Traditional Intelligence, Surveillance and Reconnaissance (NTISR) missions over Iraq using the

Outlaw Viking (BuNo. 160124), here deployed with VS-37, is being readied for a Harpoon missile shot in the Southern California (SoCal) Ops area in 1994. The aircraft was deployed from USS **Kitty Hawk** (CV-63). **Outlaw Viking** incorporated many of the over-the-horizon-targeting (OTH-T) capabilities of the P-3C **Outlaw Hunter** aircraft. (LCDR Kurt Garland, USN)

Two **Diamondcutters** from VS-30 demonstrate the considerable anti-surface capability of late-career Vikings. **Diamond** 704 in the foreground carries an AGM-65E Maverick and **Diamond** 706 carries both a Maverick and an AGM-84K SLAM-ER. The Maverick and SLAM capability were added to the Viking as part of the Maverick Plus System (MPS) upgraded in the late 1990s and early 2000s. (Jose Ramos)

A Mk 46 lightweight torpedo awaits loading onto a VS-41 Viking at NAS North Island. (Ted Carlson, Fotodynamics)

An AWW-13 pod, which provided guidance for the SLAM, was carried on the Viking's right weapons station (W6). The pod allowed the crew to guide a SLAM launched by the controlling Viking or another aircraft such as an F/A-18. The pod had a narrow transmission cone that extended forward and aft; thus, the Viking had to fly directly at or away from the target to maintain missile control. (Jose Ramos)

The Maverick/SLAM joystick controller is located on the COTACs right console and controls the laser designator. The "slew," "slave" switch, recessed (red) switch, and trigger are the only switches functional. The "coolie hat" and "pinkie" switch are disabled. (Jose Ramos)

Three S-3As drop a full load of Mk 82 500-lb bombs. It appears that the aircraft each carried three Mk 82 on each TER and four Mk 82 in the bomb bay. A maximum of 10 Mk 82 bombs could be carried, provided no retarded or Snakeye weapons were carried in the bomb bay. A retarded Mk 82 could be carried in the bomb bay provided a MAG 111 "belly band" and Mk-15 retarded fins were used to allow the weapons to clear the fuselage before fin deployment. (Robert Lawson Collection)

The LAU-117/A launch rail is used to carry and launch the AGM-65 Maverick missile. The launcher attaches to the pylon. (Jose Ramos)

A Viking from VS-38 demonstrates a defensive maneuver, breaking hard right and releasing flares from its ALE-39 dispensers. This aircraft represents the late S-3B configuration after removal of the ASW mission gear, including removal of the MAD boom and 44 of the original 60 sonobuoy chutes. (Ted Carlson, Fotodynamics)

The Mk 46 lightweight torpedo was the Viking's primary anti-ship weapon pre-S-3B years. Here a VS-32 aircraft drops a Mk 46 NEARTIP torpedo on a training exercise. The parachute retards the torpedoes descent to reduce its impact speed. (Robert Lawson Collection)

41

Three Destructor mines are mounted for mine practice in the Atlantic. Mk 80s series iron bombs could be carried on wing pylons using a Triple Ejection Rack (TER). The Destructor was a Mk 36 500-lb mine based on the Mk 82 iron bomb. The numbers represent the squadron, VS-24, and the mine identification number for recording the drop accuracy. (Author)

An S-3B from VS-33 launches a Zuni rocket from one of its port wing pods. The Viking can carry up to six of the five-inch Zuni LAU-10 (four-tube), 2.75-inch LAU-668 (seven-tube), or LAU-69 (19-tube), launchers. This launcher appears to be an LAU-69, which by the year 2000 had largely been withdrawn from use by the Viking community. (Naval Aviation Museum).

The Viking also flew Suppression of Enemy Air Defense (SEAD) missions using the ADM-141 Tactical Air-Launched Decoy (TALD). An S-3B from VS-38 (BuNo. 160580) became the first Viking to launch a TALD in combat when it launched an ADM-141 in support of Coalition air strikes on 18 January 1991. BuNo. 160585, also operating with VS-38, made the second launch a week later. The decoys, in conjunction with standoff jamming from EA-6B Prowlers, helped confuse Iraqi air-defense radars. (United States Navy)

CAPTOR mines consist of a casing containing a Mk 46 MOD 4 torpedo. Manufactured by Loral, the Mk 60 is effective as an anti-submarine weapon and also has the ability to distinguish between surface ships and submarines. Once deployed, the Mk 60 operates in a passive mode until its sensors detect a target within 3,280 feet (1,000 meters). The CAPTOR then switches to an active mode and attacks its target. (CDR Ray Ivie, USN, [Ret])

AAQ-25 LANTIRN and later the improved longer range LANTIRN-ER. VS-32's S-3Bs deployed in 2006 and 2007 with LANTIRN units and provided oversea surveillance of surface and oil platform targets in flights referenced to as Sea Dragon missions. Some Sea Dragon missions were flown with Mk 82s in the bomb bays.

Although VS-32's 2007 cruise marked the last Viking carrier deployment, VS-22 officially ended the Viking's overall employment flying LANTIRN airborne surveillance operations out of the desert. NTISR missions were flown without escort and typically with just a single fuel tank and no weapons. Overland NTISR missions were in high demand in Iraq and were able to provide either real-time relay of LANTIRN video to land stations or near-immediate viewing upon landing. While other aircraft, such as the Orion, were able to provide similar footage via their elaborate Wescam FLIRs, the Orion tapes often took nearly 23 hours to make available.

The LANTIRN-ER represented a 50-percent improvement in reliability as compared with the LANTRIN and featured doubled standoff range, a high-altitude laser, and laser spot tracker, as well as real-time geo-coordinate generator to employ GPS-guided weapons.

Three cluster-bomb units (CBU) are shown here installed on wing station W5. Cluster bombs are carried in the Mk-7 dispenser and can be used against personnel or light armor, depending on the canister load. Manufactured by ISC Technologies, the Mk-7 uses a Mk 339 time-delayed fuse, which is fused before flight and requires release at a specified altitude and airspeed to ensure proper bomblet dispersion. Although the Mk-7 can carry a variety of submunitions, Vikings rely primarily on the anti-armor Mk 20 Rockeye II, with 247 Mk 118 submunitions. Vikings also use Mk-7 dispensers loaded with the CBU-59 APAM (Anti-Personnel, Anti-Materials). This version holds 717 BLU-77 submunitions. The Mk-7 CBU-59 can be distinguished from other versions by the stenciling on the dispenser. The stencilled message reads: "Contents: (Live loaded) BLU-77/B." These dispensers are Mod 6 versions, as evidenced by their dual yellow bands, and have thermal protective covering. (Jose Ramos)

A detailed image of the AGM-65E laser-guided Maverick mounted on its LAU-117/A launch rail. The Maverick possesses a 300-lb blast/penetrating warhead and a reduced-smoke motor. It has a reported range of about 14 miles and is listed as supersonic. Over 5,000 Mavericks were launched during Desert Storm by all services. This Maverick is inert, as evidenced by the blue stripe and the lack of a tail-guidance kit. (Jose Ramos)

To expand the Viking's useful life to Battle Group Commanders, Viking crews with VS-32 experimented with the Low Altitude Navigation / Targeting Infrared (LANTIRN) pod once used by the F-14 community. The 15-inch (380mm) targeting pod, designated AN/AAQ-14, weighs about 530 lbs (240.7 kg). The LANTIRN pod system has been successfully used on the F-14 Tomcat, F-15E Strike Eagle, and F-16 Falcon. Navy Tomcats first used LANTIRN in combat during Operation Desert Fox in December 1998. (Jose Ramos)

Fleet Tanker Systems

Although the aircraft was initially configured for use as a tanker in the mid-to-late 1980s, the Viking did not assume airborne refuelling or "tanking" as an official mission until the early 1990s. The S-3A began its tanking role using the D-704 Air Refueling Store (ARS). Prototype testing was conducted on S-3A BuNo. 159749 in 1987, using the D-704 and the results were promising. Of course, these tests were different from those efforts to create a dedicated tanker, the KS-3A, which will be discussed later in this volume.

The S-3B took on a much more significant tanking role, in large part due to the departure of the A-7E and the eventual retirement of the A-6E and KA-6D in the mid-1990s. Refueling missions, whether involving mission, overhead, or recovery tanking, were performed in conjunction with other missions, taking advantage of the four-person crew and the aircraft's many sensors. Thus, a Viking might launch, top off the strike aircraft, as they existed for a strike, then perform an SSC or ASuW, or ESM mission, and then tank a flight returning as a part of recovery tanking, then land. In most missions post-1990, Vikings were the first aircraft to take off and, other than the E-2s, which were not capable of aerial refueling, the last to land.

The Viking possessed four internal fuel tanks – two feed tanks, each holding 1,200 lbs

An S-3A from VS-33 readies for in-flight refueling. The in-flight refueling probe, shown here fully extended, was mounted on the top centerline of the fuselage and could be extended/retracted electronically or manually. The probe required 70 seconds to extend or retract. When retracted, the nozzle was covered by a small hatch to reduce aerodynamic drag and to prevent probe icing. (The Robert Lawson Collection)

A detailed view shows the A/A42R-1 (31-301) aerial refueling store (ARS) Mounted on the Viking's weapon station 5, the ARS carries 265 gallons of useable fuel, or approximately 1,802 lbs of JP-5 fuel. The deck capacity of the ARS is reduced because of the 7-degree decline of the pylon store. In-flight refueling can increase the capacity to 300 gallons or 2,040-lbs of JP-5. (LCDR Tom Twomey, USN)

An Aero-1D droppable fuel tank sits affixed to the right wing station (W6) and bears the squadron name for VS-30. When airborne, the drop tank holds 300 gallons (2,040 lbs) of JP-5 fuel. Two Aero-1D tanks can be carried by the Viking. The CNU-188/A cargo pod is based on the Aero-1D. (Jose Ramos)

of JP-5 fuel, and two transfer tanks, each carrying 5,372 lbs of fuel. An additional 1,802 lbs of fuel could be carried in wing tanks (the Aero 1-D) or a combination of an Aero 1-D and an ARS. The S-3B used any of three ARS pods – the D-704, the 31-300, and the 31-301 (A/A42R-1). These refueling stores were carried on the W5 wing station and carried 1,802 lbs of fuel. The 31-300 and 31-301, which were used during the 1990s and 2000s, could offload fuel at a rate of 220 gallons per minute.

The ARS modification consisted of the following: an air refueling store, an ARS store control panel, two aircraft-mounted, electric motor-driven transfer pumps, a second bleed air select value, five additional fuses, a safety disposal switch, a green anti-collision light, a port wing tanker light, and four cockpit mirrors, two on each side of the cockpit mounted at the nine and eleven o'clock and one and three-o'clock positions.

The Viking's worth as a fleet tanker was demonstrated during Operation Desert Storm against Iraqi forces in 1991, where S-3B squadrons provided heavy tanker support for air wing assets. Aerial refueling became the aircraft's primary mission after about 1999, and this role continued until the Viking retired, although other missions were often combined with tanking to benefit the carrier battle group. The Viking's tanking mission was eventually taken over by the F/A-18E/F Super Hornet, as each air wing received its second Super Hornet squadron. As the second Super Hornet squadron arrived in the air wing, the Viking squadron was scheduled for retirement.

The Viking and Super Hornet worked well together during Operation Iraqi Freedom in 2003. Vikings performed much of the tanking around the carrier, freeing up the Super Hornets for mission tanking with the strike forces in-country, where the Vikings were more vulnerable to threats.

Aerial refueling was introduced to the Viking during themed-1980s through AFC-220. A VS-32 Mauler made history during the Gulf War as the only aircraft to use a buddy-store offensively. On 20 February 1991, Mauler 705 (BuNo. 159765) flying from USS *America* (CV-66) sank an Iraqi surface craft using three Mk 82 iron bombs and the D704 store. (Jose Ramos)

Two VS-29 Viking's demonstrate the refueling process over the Pacific. The lead Viking is likely performing a "package" check before heading off to perform its mission and taking over the refueling role from the CAG-bird. At least 80 percent of the Viking's carrier-based missions involved some transfer of fuel to other platforms. (Ted Carlson)

An S-3B launches off the USS *Theodore Roosevelt* (CVN-71) in the catapult in the Persian Gulf in October 2006. The Viking is from VS-24 and was embarked with CVW-8 aboard USS *Theodore Roosevelt* (CNV-72) Scout 700 carries a refueling store and an Aero-1D drop tank. (United States Navy)

Viking Variants

For a program that spanned an amazing 39 years, it is astonishing that only three variants of the Viking were ever fielded. This section discusses two of these variants, the US-3A Carrier On-Board Delivery (COD) aircraft and the KS-3A dedicated mission tanker. The next section discusses the S-3's major electronic surveillance variant, the ES-3A Shadow.

The US-3A COD originated from Lockheed's interest in fulfilling the Navy's need for a successor to the outdated Grumman C-1 Trader, which ironically was an off-shoot of the S-2 Tracker, which the Viking replaced. Lockheed's initial proposal called for a longer and wider aircraft based on the S-3 airframe, with a C-130-styled rear-affixed cargo door/ramp. The proposed COD variant accommodated up to 30 passengers or carried cargo, including jet engines, and could be fitted with cargo pods or fuel tanks on the wing pylons.

Lockheed's proposal was rejected, but the company persisted and reoffered a scaled-down version based on the production S-3 airframe. Lockheed converted YS-3A No. 7 (BuNo. 157998) into a US-3A prototype, removing all ASW equipment, ESM gear, and sensors, as well as any combat-related avionics. The alterations also substituted non-ejection seats for the aft cockpit and reconfigured the avionics bay to carry passengers and cargo. Lockheed replaced the APS-116 with the APS-121 color radar and an improved Loran/Omega navigation system. These modifications resulted in over 270 cubic feet of room for cargo or up to six passengers (totaling up to 4,680 lbs), in addition to the crew of three – the pilot, copilot, and cargo master. Additional cargo could be carried in specially configured wing-mounted pods.

In its basic configuration, the US-3A had a range of 2,400 nautical miles (2,760 statutory miles), which could be extended to 2,720 nautical miles (3,128 statutory miles) using two Aero-1D wing-mounted fuel tanks. The larger CNU-264 wing pods increased the total carriage to 7,400 lbs, but reduced the US-3A's range to approximately 1,920 nautical miles.

Despite its smaller size as compared with its original design, the US-3A could nevertheless carry 90 percent of the carrier's consumables, and it seemed a perfect match in terms of speed and payload for Western Pacific operations. The US-3A prototype first took to the air on 2 July 1976 and deployed aboard the USS *Kitty Hawk* (CVA-63) in the fall of 1977. Although the prototype performed well, the Navy elected to purchase a modified version of the E-2 Hawkeye, the C-2A Greyhound, for its carrier delivery mission. Small numbers of the Greyhound had been in service since the early 1960s. The Greyhound offered a larger payload and could accommodate bulkier items, such as aircraft engines.

The Navy continued to use the US-3A COD during the 1980s, and Naval Aviation Depot (NADEP), Alameda, converted five additional airframes – BuNos. 157994, 157995, 157996, 157997, and 158868. The US-3As served with VRC-50 stationed at Guam and later moved to Cubi Point in the Philippines and Diego Garcia in the Indian Ocean. BuNo. 157996 crashed in an accident off Cubi Point in 1989, while the prototype (BuNo. 157998) saw action during Operation Desert Shield/Desert Storm. The COD Viking was the sole aircraft capable of reaching carriers in the Persian Gulf from Diego Garcia. All US-3As were retired by the end of 1994 and the COD fleet accumulated some 55,000-flight hours.

The second variant was proposed as a dedicated mission tanker demonstrator. Lockheed had proposed a tanker variant with two 625-gallon tanks in the weapons bay and two 600-gallon tanks mounted on the wing, which together provided some 29,802 pounds of fuel. Refueling would take place from an aft-mounted dual internal hose and reel drogue in place of the sonobuoy chutes. Lockheed also proposed adding advanced navigation and communications gear to give the KS-3A a dual electronic warfare and communications relay capability.

In the mid-1970s, the Navy modified YS-3A No. 5 (BuNo. 157996) to demonstrate the proposed tanker configuration, adding a bolt-on belly tank and a single hose and reel drogue system. The Navy declined Lockheed's proposal and the aircraft was assigned to VS-41 for a period and in 1984 converted to a US-3A.

Further interest in a Viking tanker variant surfaced during the early 1990s with the impending retirement of the KA-6D. Unofficially termed the KS-3B, Project Sinclair called for a baseline S-3B to be stripped of all mission gear. The aircraft's avionics would likewise be modified to replace the APS-137 radar with the APS-121 radar used by the US-3A and the addition of Global Positioning System (GPS).

As the accompanying diagram illustrates, at least six configurations were evaluated. Added fuel capacities ranged from a further 1,020 lbs (75 gallons) to 6,530 lbs (480 gallons). The latter two options, options 5 and 6 which called for the addition of conformal fuel tanks, required an equipment modification to the aircraft such that it would perform one mission (ASW) or the other (tanking).

Although several fuel tank configurations were discussed, the most popular featured the installation of two 350-gallon fuel bladders in the bomb bays and two 450-gallon bladders in the avionics tunnel, thereby increasing the Viking's internal fuel to 9,750 lbs. With an external tank and aerial refueling store, the KS-3B would have carried a total of 25,894 lbs of fuel. However, because of budget constraints prevalent in the 1990s, KS-3B was never pursued.

Since the Viking's Gross Takeoff Weight (GTW) was 52,500 lbs., configurations 1, 2, and 3 each would require the Viking to launch with partially full tanks, and then top off once airborne. For example, a fully-loaded configuration option 1 (6,530 lbs.) KS-3B Viking was projected to have a GTW of 55,170 lbs. Consideration was also given to higher performance TF34 engines in order to ensure adequate performance in the event of an engine failure.

The additional service life remaining in the Viking fleet when it was retired calls into question the decision to forego a dedicated Viking tanker. A small number of KS-3B tankers aboard each carrier would free up a number of Super Hornets for strike missions.

This represents a unique photo showing the two Viking prototypes under consideration in the late 1970s. In the forefront is the baseline S-3A Viking with its ASQ-81(V) MAD boom extended. A US-3A Carrier Onboard Delivery (COD) prototype holds formation off the Viking's right wing, with a large CNU-264/A cargo pod prominent on its left wing station. The KS-3A demonstrator is in the background, its refueling drogue deployed. (Robert Lawson Collection)

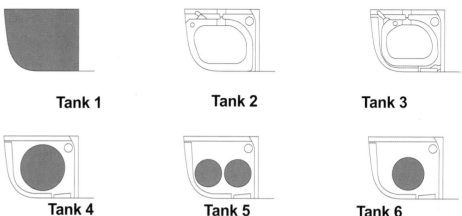

Tank 1 **Tank 2** **Tank 3**

Tank 4 **Tank 5** **Tank 6**

A mid-1990s proposal (Project Sinclair) calling for a KS-3B tanker failed to gain footing and was never pursued. Several possible configurations were studied, including one (shown in Tank Configuration 1) which included an integral tanking requiring a dedicated aircraft. Tank Configuration proposals 2-6 would have left the Viking's ASW mission gear intact and gave squadron commanders the option of reconfiguring the aircraft for tanking or standard Viking missions. Tank Configuration 1 provided the largest carriage of 480 gallons (6,530-lbs) of fuel. (Lockheed Martin)

The CNU-264/A cargo pod was carried by all US-3A COD aircraft and an occasional S-3A/B. The CNU-264/A cargo pod enabled US-3A's to haul an additional 1,000 lbs of cargo. A smaller CNU-188/A pod was also available and could carry up to 350 lbs. Project Gray Wolf used a CNU-264/A pod modified with an F-4 Phantom II nose cone to house the Westinghouse Systems APG-76 SAR radar. (S-3 NATOPS Manual)

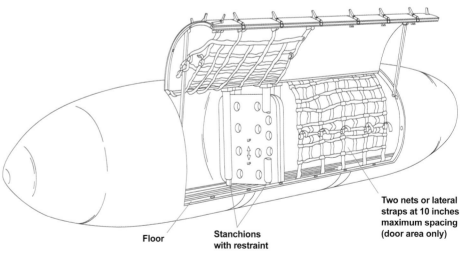

Floor — Stanchions with restraint — Two nets or lateral straps at 10 inches maximum spacing (door area only)

The KS-3A demonstrator (BuNo. 157996) refuels the US-3A prototype (BuNo. 157998) The KS-3A demonstrator operated with VS-41 and was eventually converted to a US-3A. It crashed in the water on approach to NAS Cubi Point in the Philippines on 20 January 1989. (Robert Lawson Collection)

The KS-3A demonstrator refuels an A-7E Corsair II. The demonstrator did not use a buddy store but instead had a drogue and reel system installed into the bomb bay area, thereby permitting the aircraft to carry two Aero-1D drop tanks. (Robert Lawson Collection)

The US-3A prototype was the seventh pre-production flight test aircraft and in that capacity flew missions evaluating weapons systems. Note the US-3A has an extra window just aft of the cockpit glass. (Robert Lawson Collection)

VS-33 took the US-3A prototype of their 1977-78 WestPac cruise aboard USS *Kitty Hawk* (CV-63), marking the COD's first deployment. Six of the US-3As were constructed and deployed with VFC-50 in the Western pacific. (The Robert Lawson Collection)

ES-3A Shadow

The ES-3A Shadow is the most well-known and significant variant of the S-3 Viking. Entering service in the early 1990s, the Shadow actually originated in a 1977 Lockheed proposal called Tactical Airborne Signal Exploitation System (TASES) to develop an electronic warfare variant. TASES proposed replacing the Viking's ASW mission gear with sophisticated surveillance and monitoring equipment that would allow the variant to replace the electronic warfare EA-3A Whale, itself a variant of the A-3D Skywarrior. One Viking, No. 158868, was modified to TASES standards in 1981.

While the Navy did not pursue TASES, the study laid the foundation for what would become the ES-3A some ten years later. Lockheed revisited the proposal and by 1989, it was agreed that a total of sixteen S-3s would be converted to the new electronic warfare variant under a $500 million contract. Lockheed utilized aircraft 3000, the original "Lifetime Stress Simulation Aircraft," to serve as a static mockup and converted YS-3A No. 2 (BuNo. 157993) to an ES-3A to serve as an aerodynamic prototype, allowing flight tests of the new configuration. The aerodynamic prototype carried no mission avionics, its antennas only non-functional mock-ups. Ballast was placed throughout the mock-up to simulate weight, loading, and center of gravity.

The ES-3A prototype (BuNo. 159401) first flew on 15 May 1991. Flight tests were performed by both Lockheed and the Navy, the latter focusing on flutter and loads on the aircraft's tail. Engineers were concerned that changes in airflow might alter the air loads on the horizontal and vertical stabilizers, but the tests were negative. Carrier testing occurred in 1990-91 at NAS Patuxent River using a C-7 catapult and arresting gear followed by instrumentation testing to provide a baseline for the mission avionics.

Structural modifications removed all of the Viking's ASW mission gear, including sonobuoy launchers and the MAD. The twin bomb bays were removed and replaced with equipment racks for "black boxes" and mission avionics for its electronic warfare role. A new cooling system, the Vapor Cycle System (VCS), was installed to provide air conditioning for the new electronics in the bay and to sanitize moisture and salt from the aircraft to reduce corrosion. Externally, 63 new antennas were installed, most noticeably the so-called upper and lower canoe housing and the doomed antennas, which contain the spinning directional-finding OE-320 antennas.

The Shadow retained the Viking's FLIR and APS-137 radar. Communications and navigation were upgraded, with the Shadow receiving the ARC-182/-187 UHF/VHF radios, AN/ASN-92 CAINS II, SATCOM, Omega, and Navstar GPS. The aircraft's ESM suite was also modified, adding a manually operated AN/ALR-81 and the ULQ-16(V) (2) Three AYK-14 computers replaced the AYK-10. Finally, the Shadow incorporated the Multi-Static Processor (MPS), which gave the ES-3A a passive airborne exploitation capability in the same league as the larger EP-3E and the RC-135 Rivet Joint.

A colorful shot of the ES-3A aerodynamic prototype's maiden flight. Many of the Shadow's 63 antennae are visible. Modifications to the ES-3A prototype were completed in 1989. Sixteen S-3A were converted to the ES-3A design in a three-phase conversion program conducted at Hanger 14 at NAS Cecil Field, Florida. (LCDR Richard B. Burgess, USN. [Ret])

Fleet Reconnaissance Squadron Five (VQ-5) was originally established at NAS Agana, Guam, but later moved to NAS North Island in 1994. VQ-5 Sea Shadows served the West Coast air wings and a two-plane detachment (Det 5) was established in Japan as part of forward-deployed CVW-5. This Shadow is performing a secondary surveillance mission, as evidenced by its deployed FLIR. (CAPT Chris Buhlmann, USNR)

The Shadow's cockpit was also renovated, with a variety of state-of-the-art color touch-sensitive displays and system interfaces. Most notably, the COTAC's station was modified such that all of the flight controls were replaced with mission-specific gear. New communications, GPS navigation, an enhanced ESM suite, and upgraded computers (indeed, three new AYK-14 models) were also added to handle the additional processing needs.

The Shadows crew differed from that of the Viking. The ES-3A pilot served as the overall electronic warfare (EW) commander, a Naval Flight Officer (NFO) replaced the COTAC and served as the EW Combat Coordinator (EWCC), and two enlisted EW specialists filled the back seats, either an EW operator (EWOPS) or a cryptologist technician (CTI) or both. The pilot or the NFO served as Mission Commander responsible for the overall mission. Shadow squadrons typically deployed with eight or nine officers and 45 enlisted personnel.

The overall modifications added approximately 4,000 pounds of weight and significantly increased the aircraft's draft, making it a slower and less responsive aircraft versus the S-3B. Range is also reduced versus the Viking, as is the Shadow's maximum design load factor, 3.1 compared to 3.5 Gs of the S-3B. The additional electronics also shifted the aircraft's center of gravity forward slightly, but not so as to cause concern.

Field conversations took place at Hanger 14, belonging to VS-27, at NAS Cecil Field in four stages, with a new ES-3A emerging every six months. The modifications have been described by some as the most complex field modification program every undertaken.

The ES-3A flew a host of electronic surveillance missions ranging from Electronic Intelligence (ELINT), Communications Intelligence (COMINT), and Signal Intelligence (SIGINT), as well as complementary missions consisting of Overland Battle Damage Assessment (OBDA), Over-the-Horizon Targeting (OTH-T), and tanking. Shadows provided the Carrier Battle Group with an organic electronic reconnaissance capability and allowed Commanders to obtain a complete electronic order of battle (EOB). The Shadows' passive sensors permitted detection and location of communications centers, radars, missile sites, and AAA batteries, as well as determining emissions from aircraft and surface ships. Shadows from both VQ squadrons were especially active during Operation Southern Watch over Iraq and ES-3As from VQ-6 flew support during the mid-1990s Bosnia and Kosovo air campaigns in the Adriatic Sea.

Typically Shadows flew missions at high-altitudes at long standoff range, gathering information about enemy air defense networks, listening to communications, and helping identify and classify potential targets. Shadows often worked together with S-3Bs to create an overall electronic order of battle. Due to the limited number of ES-3As in the detachment, Shadows would often fly a mission along a designated route, followed by an S-3B Viking using its ESM suite and then compared data obtained from the two flights before making a second Shadow flight where the ES-3A could fine-tune the observations.

ES-3As began deploying to the fleet in May 1992, with a single squadron established on each coast. VQ-5 Sea Shadows based at NAS Agana, Guam, (later moved to NAS North Island in October 1994) served West Coast air wings and VQ-6 Black Ravens

An ES-3A reveals its tops side antennas. The black blade antenna (ahead of the canoe) is the ALD-9 (HF-DF) antenna. The "dome" structure houses the ALR-81 antenna and the "whip" is the RFD antenna. A VOR/GS antenna can be seen on the fin above the squadron marking and the rectangular ALD-9 "ferrite loop" antenna extends from the aircraft's tail section where the MAD would be on the S-3A/B. (CAPT Chris Buhlmann, USNR)

served East Coast air wings, basing out of NAS Cecil Field. Shadow 159403, the first to complete the modifications, joined VQ-5 on 8 May 1992. VQ-5 had been established in August 1991 and had been given two S-3s from VS-29 (BuNos. 159406 and 159739) to use for pilot and crew training until their full complement of Shadows arrived.

Shadows deployed in small two plane detachments called DETs. One VQ-5 Detachment, called Det 5, was permanently deployed to NAF Misawa, Japan, as part of CVW-5. The first ES-3A operational carrier deployment began in April 1993 aboard USS *Independence* (CV-62) VQ-6 made the first East Coast ES-3A operational deployment in January 1994 aboard USS *Saratoga* (CV-60) The last of the 16 ES-3As was delivered on 30 September.

Det 11 (formerly Det D) made VQ-5's last deployment aboard USS *Vinson* (CVN-70) in December 1998 supporting Operation Desert Fox. VQ-6 made a total of 13 major deployments, including operations in support of NATO missions in Bosnia. The final VQ-6 deployment was conducted by Det A aboard USS *Enterprise* (CVN-65) in Operation Desert Fox.

Due to costs and budgetary constraints, the Shadows were retired in May 1999, leaving Carrier Battle Groups to depend on land-based electronic surveillance resources, such as the EP-3E Aries II. The last ES-3A (BuNo.159752) arrived at AMARC on 10 August 1999 and was placed in Type 1000 storage, where it could be regenerated for war service, if needed. Beginning in 2003, however, the Shadows were moved to the reclamation area, where they provided parts to fleet units. Upgrades to the Shadow's ELINT/SIGINT capabilities were considered under the designation Viking Watch/Shadow Box, but no details are available.

The Shadow cockpit is much different that the S-3B. Most notable are the larger displays and the absence of a flight control stick for the EWCC (the COTAC in the Viking); there is also no display for the pilot. A CAINS II navigation system, which was later incorporated into the S-3B (see page 59), is seen on the center console. (Jose Ramos)

Although BuNo. 157993 was the ES-3A aerodynamic prototype, BuNo. 159401 was the first operational prototype. It later flew with VQ-6 based at NAS Cecil Field. BuNo. 159404 (which flew with VQ-5) one was the first production ES-3A. (LCDR Richard B. Burgess, USN. [Ret.])

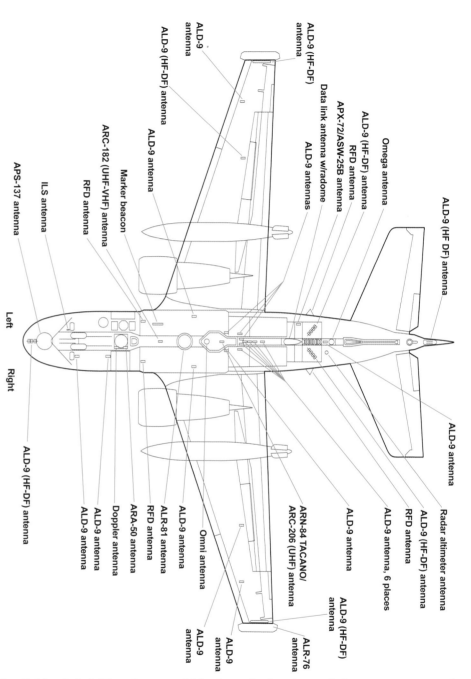

The S-3A carried 63 antennas which dramatically changed the appearance and aerodynamics of the core Viking. The long dorsal hump is often referred to as the "canoe." (ES-3A NATOPS Manual)

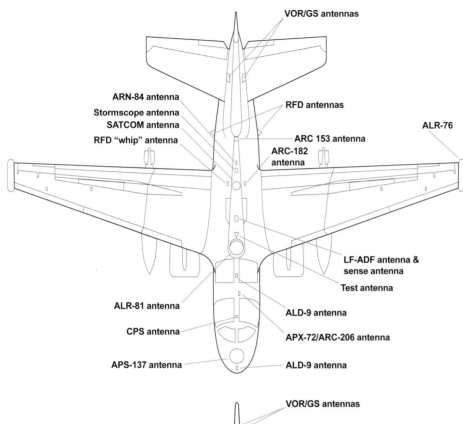

VOR/GS antennas

ARN-84 antenna
Stormscope antenna
SATCOM antenna
RFD "whip" antenna

RFD antennas

ARC 153 antenna

ARC-182 antenna

ALR-76

LF-ADF antenna &
sense antenna

Test antenna

ALR-81 antenna

ALD-9 antenna

CPS antenna

APX-72/ARC-206 antenna

APS-137 antenna

ALD-9 antenna

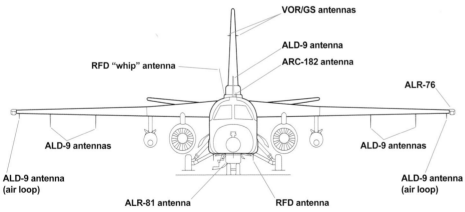

VOR/GS antennas

ALD-9 antenna

ARC-182 antenna

RFD "whip" antenna

ALR-76

ALD-9 antennas

ALD-9 antennas

ALD-9 antenna
(air loop)

ALD-9 antenna
(air loop)

ALR-81 antenna

RFD antenna

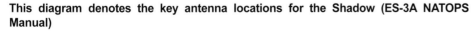

This diagram denotes the key antenna locations for the Shadow (ES-3A NATOPS Manual)

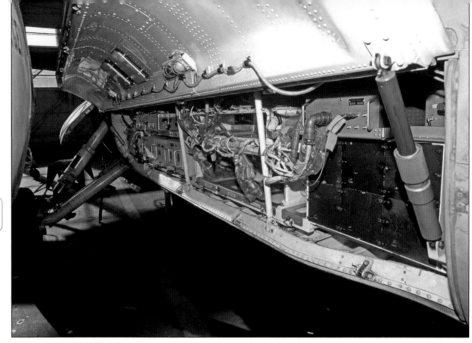

The S-3A bomb bay was reconfigured to accommodate the Shadow's electronics and avionics boxes to support its clandestine missions. (Jose Ramos)

Located on each side of the Shadow just ahead of the "Navy" marking is the APX-72/ASW-25B cone antenna, referred to as the "Madonna" antenna. (Jose Ramos)

The Electronic Warfare Operator (EWOP) station replaced the S-3A SENSO station. Shown here are the updated liquid crystal displays (LCD) and the new video recorders. (Jose Ramos)

The TACCO station of the Viking was modified for a second EWOP or a CTI, depending on the mission. ES-3As used CTIs, or cryptologist, heavily during operations supporting flights over Bosnia. (Jose Ramos)

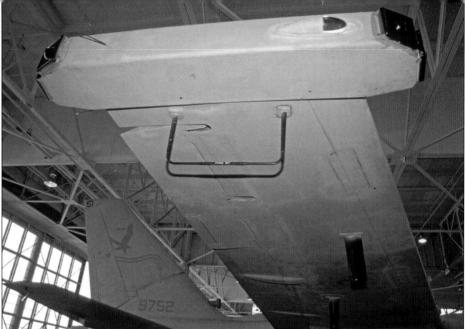

The Shadow's 63 antennas are largely visible here, especially the bottom grouping. The long rectangle just aft of the ALQ-81 dome is the ARN-84/ARC-204 TACAN/UHF antenna. Located on it is a small conical omni antenna, followed by several ALD-9 antennas. (Jose Ramos)

A VQ-5 ES-3A flies above one of the Forrestal-class carriers. The two large blades on the lower wing surface are ALD-9 antennas; the ALD-9 (HD-DF) loop antenna is also visible near the ALR-76 receiver. The ES-3A carried highly sensitive, full-threat spectrum RF receivers, directional finding antennas, and recording gear, allowing information to be received and relayed back to the carrier. (LCDR Richard B. Burgess, USN. [Ret])

A close-up of this VQ-6 aircraft reveals the ALD-9 (HD-DF) "loop" antenna. This "loop" was sometimes removed and shortened due to cracking problems discovered during carrier deployments. (Jose Ramos)

A VQ-5 Shadow appears in more colorful markings. Note the "CITGO" emblem on the buddy store reflecting the significant tanking role played by the Shadow. The ES-3A, manned by a crew of four, replaced the EA-3B *Skywarrior* (also called Whale) which had a crew of seven. Shadows typically deployed in detachments of two aircraft and, while deployed, often assumed the carrier air wing markings of its parent air wing. (Jose Ramos)

Viking and Shadow Squadrons

The S-3 Viking has been operated exclusively by the U.S. Navy. Over the years there have been 14 S-3A/B Viking squadrons, including two Fleet Readiness Squadrons (FRS), plus two VQ squadrons operating the ES-3A Shadow. Vikings also flew with VX-1 and the Naval Air Warfare Center, Aircraft Division, at NAS Patuxent River, Maryland.

East Coast S-3 squadrons were based at NAS Cecil Field, Florida, until 1997, when they relocated to NAS Jacksonville, Florida. East Coast S-3s are controlled by the Sea Control Wing, U.S. Atlantic Fleet, which was established in 1973 as Air Anti-Submarine Warfare Wing and later redesignated Sea Strike Wing One (1987-1992). VS-27, which served as the S-3B FRS from 1987 until September 1994, operated within SeaConWingLant, as did a Special Projects Division, the Sea Control Weapons School, VQ-6, and the S-3 Tactical Support Center.

West Coast S-3 squadrons, under the command of Sea Control Wing, U.S. Pacific Fleet, were based at NAS North Island, California. VQ-5 and VS-41, the original S-3 FRS and later sole FRS, were also based at North Island. VS-21 and a detachment of VQ-5 were forward deployed with Air Wing Five at NAF Atsugi and Misawa, Japan. SeaConWingPac also operated a Special Projects Division.

Vikings deployed with the 7XX Modex, while VQ-5 Shadows deployed with 72X, and VQ-6 Shadows deployed with 76X. Tail codes varied according to air wing assignment; however, VS-27 displayed "AD" and VS-41 "NJ" markings. The ES-3A squadrons were initially assigned "SS" for VQ-5 and "ET" for VQ-6, but typically adopted the code of their deployed air wing. Each deployment was also designated with a Detachment letter; some were later redesignated with the assigned air wing (such as Det 11). COD Vikings served with VRC-50 *Foo Dogs,* bore the "RG" tail code, while VX-1 carried "JA."

Vikings were not assigned to reserve air wings. During the 1980s, personnel from the Reserve Squadron Augment Unit (SAU) served with VS-0174 at NAS Cecil Field and VS-0294 at NAS North Island. A Viking Support Unit (VSSU) also operated S-3s and later became VS-27 on 21 January 1987. With no aircraft of its own, the VSSU operated as part of the FRS and provided aircraft access for reserve pilots, crews, and mechanics.

VS-35 had multiple lives with the Viking. The squadron, then known as the *Boomerangers,* established with the S-3A in March 1987, deploying with CVW-10 from 24 July through 5 August 1987 aboard USS *Enterprise* (CVN-65) for a short EastPac cruise. The squadron disestablished, but was reformed as the *Blue Wolves* in April 1991, flying the S-3B.

VQ-5 was established at NAS Agana, Guam, on 15 August 1991, and was disestablished on 4 June 1999. When Agana was closed in 1994, VQ-5 moved to NAS North Island in San Diego, California, and Detachment 5, which permanently operated with Carrier Air Wing 5, relocated to NAF Misawa, Japan. VQ-6 was established at NAS Cecil Field, Florida, on 26 August 1991.

VRC-50's *Foo Dogs* operated six US-3A beginning in the early 1980s until August 1994. Vikings also operated with VX-1 *Pioneers* from early 1974 until September 2004 and with VX-20 Force from July 1996 though April 2004.

A clean-lined VS-32 S-3A cruises over the Atlantic. The *Maulers* transitioned to the S-3A from the S-2G in October 1975. VS-32 was the first S-3A squadron to log more than 1,000 flight hours while deployed without missing a sortie. After transitioning to the Bravo, the squadron became the first to fly the Viking overland in support of UN/NATO Deny Flight operations in Bosnia. (LCDR Richard B. Burgess, USN. [Ret])

A flight of S-3B Vikings over northern Florida highlight a collection of CAG-birds from VS-24, VS-30, VS-31 and VS-32. Modex 702 is from VS-32 *Checkmates.* (Jose Ramos)

Modex 705 sets ready for launch on Number 4 port side catapult. The air wing is CVW-11, a West Coast air wing. This Viking has a buddy-store and an Aero-1D drop tank. (Jose Ramos)

This excellent close-up of an S-3B shows the paint scheme around the cockpit area. The yellow strip on the leading edge of the wing is a stall strip. The windshield wipers are also plainly visible as is the small box diagram just above the windshield, which marks the door enclosing the refueling probe. (CAPT Chris Buhlmann, USNR)

An S-3B in a sharp right bank reveals its open bomb bays and also highlights the sonobuoy chutes following the removal of the aircraft's ASW equipment in 1999. The vacated MAD boom is prominent. This perspective provides a good view of the third ALE-39 dispenser located on the bottom of the aircraft just forward of the sonobuoy chute. (CAPT Chris Buhlmann, USNR)

Originally YS-3A Number 6 (BuNo. 157997), this VRC-50 *Foo Dogs* US-3A bears the name "City of Oakland" on its radome. As a flight test aircraft, this Viking performed armament, weapons, and avionics integration testing. (Robert Lawson Collection)

The VSSU were supplemental units providing additional crews for the Viking community. (Robert Lawson Collection)

The small hand-held device is known as Pandora's Box and allowed Viking crews to monitor communications using "common-off-the-shelf" (COTS) technology and an installed ALD-9 antenna. This program, as well as several other similar projects (Thunderbird and Hound Dog), were attempts to recapture some of the mission lost when the Shadow was retired. (Jose Ramos)

Viking Squadrons

Designation	Name	To S-3A	To S-3B	Fleet
VS-21	Fighting Red Tails	1974	1990	P
VS-22	Checkmates	1975	1989	A
VS-24	Scouts	1975	1989	A
VS-27	Sea Wolfs	----	1987	A
VS-28	Gamblers	1975	1990	A
VS-29	Dragonfires	1975	1992	P
VS-30	Diamondcutters	1977	1988	A
VS-31	Topcats	1976	1989	A
VS-32	Maulers	1975	1990	A
VS-33	Screwbirds	1976	1992	P
VS-35	Boomerangers	1987	----	P
VS-35	Blue Wolves	----	1991	P
VS-37	Sawbucks	1976	1992	P
VS-38	Red Griffins	1976	1993	P
VS-41	Shamrocks	1974	1990	P

1990s and the 21st Century

With the end of the Cold War in 1991, and the new capabilities demonstrated by the Viking during the Gulf War, the S-3B found itself in an awkward position. The primary purpose for which it had been built – combating Soviet submarines – was now a significantly diminished threat. However, the Viking and its entrepreneurial crews had demonstrated that the platform was capable of many more tasks, if only adequate funding were available. By 1992, nominal 10-plane Viking squadrons had been reduced to six aircraft each, but were then increased to eight Vikings, as airframes began assuming some of the roles of the departing A-6E Intruders.

As the 1990s progressed, the Viking assumed the role of the carrier air wing's organic tanker, ultimately replacing the KA-6D, which retired in 1996. Vikings performed valuable overhead and recovery tanking, as well as mission tanking when the aircraft could be stationed out of potential threat areas. As the decade continued, the Viking's missions navigated away from the ASW mission, which was now being assumed by a combination of ship-based sensors, Seahawks, and where possible, land-based P-3C Orions. As a result, beginning in 1999 (and as part of AFC 284), the aircraft's MAD boom, 44 of its 60 sonobuoy chutes, and all acoustic processing equipment were removed, resulting in weight savings of over 834 lbs per aircraft. Aircrews were reduced to three members with the elimination of the SENSO. VS-32 was the last squadron to have its ASW gear removed in 2000 and VS-24 was the first squadron to deploy without a SENSO.

Yet at about the same time, the S-3B was receiving new capabilities to enhance its performance of surface missions. In 1997 and 1998, four Atlantic Fleet Vikings were modified to accommodate AGM-65F Infrared (IR) Maverick missiles as part of a proof-of-concept project to demonstrate the aircraft's littoral strike potential. These four aircraft cross decked among with several VS squadrons, with VS-22 being the first to deploy what eventually became known as the Maverick Plus System (MPS). Officially designated as AN/AGM-32(V2), MPS offered full targeting, launch, and control capability of the AGM-65E Laser and AGM-65F IR Maverick and (in conjunction with a wing-mounted AWW-13 extended-range data-link pod) the AGM-84H/K SLAM-ER missile. Forty aircraft were eventually converted MPS Vikings. Two other additions as part of the MPS included new Active Matrix Liquid Crystal Display (AMLCD) monitors for the cockpit and the MIL-STD-1553 bus. The pilot's monitor was replaced with a 6-by-8-inch display; the COTAC's monitor was slightly larger, and two 17-inch AMLCD monitors were installed in the aft seats.

At about the same time, a program known as the Surveillance System Upgrade (SSU) commenced, with the goal of enabling the Viking's ability to transmit real-time tactical data. Beginning in the summer of 1999, SSU proceeded on a dual-track program, with the Sea Control Wing Atlantic studying an advanced long-range electro-optical/infrared (EO/IR) sensor and a real-time data link, and the Sea Control Wing Pacific testing an ultra high-resolution Synthetic Aperture Radar (SAR) radar, the APS-137C(V)5, based in part on the Gray Wolf demonstrator. The new radar was coupled with the Link-16 Joint Tactical Distribution System (JTIDS), a Real-Time Sensor Data Link (RTSDL), and a

A Maverick-Plus (MPS) S-3B from VS-29 carries a SLAM-ER and an AWW-13 data link pod as it prosecutes an attack against a land-based target. (CAPT Chris Buhlmann, USNR)

new AYK-23 digital computer.

The SSU Viking first deployed with VS-35 aboard USS *Abraham Lincoln* (CVN-72), and later deployed with VS-24 and VS-29, the latter in the Persian Gulf. The SSU Viking was reportedly the "most sought after asset in the theater." VS-29 reported that the SSU aircraft, BuNo, 159766, flew 115 of the squadron's sorties, including 60 missions over Iraq.

Although the SSU project ended due to a lack of funding, several other modifications were made to the Viking as part of a critical avionics upgrade program, touching on navigation, communications, and computer processing. Between 1998 and 2003, the various update programs saw installation of the Carrier Airborne Inertial Navigation System II (CAINS II) and Global Positioning Systems, as well as the CP-1074B AN/ASW-33 digital flight data computer, and the AYK-23 digital computer. Larger LCD displays – the so-called "glass cockpit" – were also installed, which greatly improved the data displays. There have been comments, however, that the response time was not as rapid as the older CRTs, which made on-screen detection of smaller objects, such as periscopes, more difficult. The Communications Improvement Program (CIP) update, which began in 1998, also brought installation of new radios capable of six-digit transmission, which also introduced the SATCOM and ARC-210 HAVEQUICK.

One of the more significant modifications involved the addition of the Mass Memory Unit, which replaced the S-3B memory unit. The MMU contained a removable memory card, a 14-Gigabyte flash drive, which allowed crews to program all preflight data on a laptop and then download the information once aboard the Viking. Flight data could also be stored on the MMU and removed after flight for further analysis.

Ironically, Lockheed testing conducted during the early 2000s demonstrated that initial assessments of the Viking's fatigue life were greatly understated. Completed in 2004, Lockheed's Full-Scale Fatigue Test showed that the Viking's service life could be as great as 23,000 flight hours. At the time, most Viking's averaged around 13,000, still shy of the original projections of 15,000 flight hours. Despite these figures, the Viking was set for retirement.

In 2006, the Viking saw its last major upgrade with the addition of a wing-mounted AAQ-25 Low-Altitude Navigation Targeting Infrared for Night (LANTIRN) pod left over from the retired F-14 program. Attempting to fill the void for airborne overland surveillance, the Viking community via VS-32's Maulers modified a Viking (BuNo. 159744), installing the LANTIRN on the aircraft's right wing station, and altering the COTACT station with a joystick to control the device.

VS-32 deployed with the LANTIRN prototype over Southern Iraq in the summer of 2006 and it quickly proved its worth, flying 47 NTISR missions, totaling 180 flight hours in support of British and Australian troops. A second LANTIRN Viking, BuNo. 160599, was being tested back at NAS Patuxent River. Twelve S-3Bs were subsequently modified to carry and operate LANTIRN. VS-31 and -32 deployed the LANTIRN on their final missions, and a detachment of four VS-22 Vikings took an enhanced Extended Range (ER) version to Iraq, marking the final S-3B deployment. These four Vikings also received a communications modification, adding the PRC-117 U/VHF radio for easier

The Viking received a significant navigation upgrade via the CAINS II navigation system shown here in the center of the photo. Originally installed on the ES-3A, the CAINS II greatly improved navigation for Viking crews. (Jose Ramos)

The pilot's station received a new six-by-eight inch liquid crystal display (LCD) as part of the Maverick Plus upgrade during the late 1990s. (Jose Ramos)

The AN/AAQ-25 LANTIRN pod was adapted for the Viking by members of VS-32 and VX-1 in late 2005. This pod hangs on wing station six on the second prototype aircraft, BuNo. 160599, at the time deployed with VS-31. (Jose Ramos)

The LANTIRN controller is located at the COTAC station just forward of the Maverick/SLAM controller joystick. The COTAC computer tray was removed to accommodate a modified LANTIRN Control Panel (LCP). (Jose Ramos)

communications with ground forces.

A Viking follow-on aircraft was explored beginning in 1993 under the name of the Common Support Aircraft (CSA). The proposal, evaluated by Lockheed Martin, sought to combine the mission areas of the E-2C, EA-6B, S-3B, ES-3A, and the C-2A into a single common airframe, incorporating many of the systems already used by the Viking and Shadow or tested in the Viking proof-of-concept demonstrators. The CSA was to include state-of-the-art electronics and incorporate high-resolution SAR/ISAR radar with GMTI capability, and be crewed by four. Lockheed's CSA-101 proposal, considered its low-risk alternative, had a strong resemblance to the Viking. CSA-201 incorporated limited low-observability features such as faceted airframe and AESA radar. CSA-301, the stealthiest of the proposals under consideration, offered full low-observability and incorporated conformal sensor arrays into the leading and trailing edges of the diamond-shaped planform. The first phase of the study lasted two years and was completed in 1997. When conceived the program was to deliver a production aircraft in 2009 and achieve IOC in 2013. CSA was canceled in 1999.

With the exit of the Viking, ASW duties are handled by a combination of ship-based systems, the HH-60R, and land-based Orions, while tanking mission has been assumed by the F/A-18E/F Super Hornet. Although the Super Hornet has likewise taken over the Viking's SUW duties, it lacks the ISAR capability of the APS-137.

An S-3B from the Fleet Replacement Squadron, VS-41, is about to touch down at NAS North Island, California. (MC 1 Alan Warner, U.S. Navy)

The Common Support Aircraft (CSA) was to provide a follow-on to the Viking. This artists' rendition from Lockheed Martin shows an AEW and ASuW variant operating from the USS *Ronald Reagan* (CVN-76) The CSA was cancelled in 1999 due to budgetary constraints and its mission migrated to other platforms such as the FA-18E/F Super Hornet and the MH-60R Seahawk. (Lockheed Martin)

Four of the remaining Vikings are now with NASA's Glenn Research Center in Ohio, where they are being used for anti-icing studies. (CAPT Chris Buhlmann, USNR)

The Viking at War

Much of the Viking's Cold War years were spent flying in support of its primary ASW mission. Viking's deployed with every carrier air wing in 10-aircraft squadrons. Plans called for a surge to 20 aircraft for special threat areas, such as the GIUK Gap, by shifting assets from non-deployed carriers or those operating in lower-threat regions. During these years, Vikings flew missions armed with a combination of torpedoes, depth bombs, and a single fuel tank, and concentrated on a combination of surface search and ASW missions. Approximately 65 percent of all S-3A missions flown during this era were ASW. Beginning in 1984, Vikings also began carrying D-704 refueling stores, and by 1987 were routinely flying tanking missions, assisting KA-6D and KA-7E tankers.

Operation Desert Storm in 1991 ushered in a new era for the Viking, as crews sought to expand the aircraft's role in the air wing based on the aircraft's inherent and yet untested capabilities. Using innovative weapons loads and improvised tactics, Vikings flew electronic warfare, in-flight refueling, ASW, airborne command/control, combat surveillance, anti-surface warfare, mine surveillance, airborne counter-targeting, cruise-missile countermeasures, and SAR coordination missions.

When Iraq invaded Kuwait on 2 August 1990, Vikings aboard USS *Independence* (CV-62) and USS *Eisenhower* (CVN-69) flew surface interdiction and electronic intelligence collection missions, taking advantage of the S-3's sophisticated radar and ESM suites to help develop an accurate electronic order of battle. One of these squadrons, VS-30, was stationed in the eastern Mediterranean and the Red Sea, and flew combat surveillance missions, fixing electronic locations and collecting possible targets for use in future operations. Deploying aboard USS *Saratoga* (CV-60), the *Diamondcutters*, which were on station from August 1990 through March 1991, totaled over 4,000 flight hours and 1,160 sorties (258 combat sorties) and recorded over 1,000 traps.

Vikings also scored a number of "firsts" during the war, marking the first launch of an ADM-141 Tactical Air-Launched Decoy (TALD) (by VS-38), destroying an Iraqi AAA site with Mk-82 bombs (by VS-24), and sinking an Iraqi patrol boat (by VS-24 and -32). VS-22 also made extensive use of its FLIR, ESM, and APS-137 ISAR in overland radar and Scud-hunting and tactical ELINT sorties. VS-22 flew 1,100 combat hours in 324 combat sorties in direct support of Coalition Forces. The *Checkmates* also flew a considerable number of ASW missions, spending over 200 hours tracking Russian submarines in the Mediterranean Sea.

A total of 41 Vikings from seven different squadrons flew in Desert Shield/Desert Storm, flying 1,674 combat sorties and delivering over 2.5 million gallons of fuel. Five East Coast squadrons (VS-22, -24, -30, -31, -32) flew the S-3B and two West Coast squadrons (VS-37 and –38), flew the S-3A. All Vikings returned home safely.

Despite the fact that Viking squadrons were often the smallest sized aboard the carriers, crews logged significant statistics. For example, VS-38 flew 554 sorties for a total of 1,428.1 flight hours; VS-24 flew 449 sorties and 990 flight hours. In total, over 2.4 million gallons of fuel were passed by Vikings during the Storm. The success of Viking operations during the Gulf War laid the foundation for many of the proof-of-concept

A VS-37 S-3B loaded with TALD is being preflighted here for a Missile Exercise (MissilEx) in the Western pacific in 1994. TALD was used in a deceptive role to either mask strike aircraft as they ingressed a target area or to simulate an aircraft strike profile so as to trick enemy air defense radars into tracking the TALD and revealing their location. (LCDR Kurt Garland)

The ES-3A provided an organic electronic intelligence capability to carrier battle groups that is sorely missed today, as fleet commanders must rely on a limited number of heavily tasked EP-3E Aries II to fill the mission gap. (Jose Ramos)

aircraft that emerged in the mid-to-late 1990s, such as Maverick Viking, SSU Viking, and Outlaw Viking.

Vikings also played a critical role in UN air operations around Bosnia and Kosovo in 1996 and 1999 respectively, flying electronic reconnaissance and Armed Surface Reconnaissance (ARS) missions, as well as performing tanking missions. Many squadrons saw heavy usage, sometimes seeing as many as 2,000 flight hours over the course of deployments. VS-30, for example, logged over 2,000 flight hours and 950 traps during their 1999-99 Adriatic/Persian Gulf deployment aboard USS *Eisenhower* (CVN-69) *Diamondcutters* flew tanking and ARS missions featuring the new Maverick-capable Vikings.

Combat operations again followed in 2001 during Operation Enduring Freedom (OEF, Afghanistan) and in 2003 during Operation Iraqi Freedom (OIF) One of the highlights of the Viking's operations was the airframes first combat launch of a laser-guided Maverick. On 25 March 2003, an S-3B from VS-38 launched a Maverick against an Iraqi naval target in the Tigris River, damaging the vessel. Viking's also flew extensive tanker support, with some squadrons seeing as many as 30 missions a day. Many of the Viking's OEF and OIF missions involved tanking.

The final Viking combat cruise was conducted by VS-32 *Maulers* aboard USS *Enterprise* (CVN-65) Beginning in July 2007, VS-32 provided support for Carrier Air Wing One (CVW-1). The squadron concluded its deployment in December 2007.

During 2007, VS-22, although not deploying aboard a carrier, made three deployments to Curacao, Netherlands Antilles, in support of Joint Interagency Task Force South counter-narcotics operations.

The Viking ended its combat career flying land-based missions out of al-Asad Air Base, in al-Anbâr province, Iraq. In July 2008, four LANTIRN-equipped S-3Bs from VS-22 (BuNos. 159746, 160147, 160581, and 160601) deployed to Iraq to conduct Non-Traditional Intelligence, Surveillance, and Reconnaissance (NTISR) missions against insurgents. A total of 120 personnel, including aircrews and maintenance personnel made the deployment. LT Tom Genest, who deployed with VS-22, said that the Viking LANTIRN's proved extremely valuable in counter-Improvised Explosive Devices (IEDs) efforts and flew a variety of reconnaissance missions for convoys searching for IEDs. Vikings were also used to monitor border crossings and target development. LT Genest commented that the Viking performed well and experienced few mechanical problems, which came as a surprise given the heavy sand environment of the desert. Overall, the four Vikings flew over 1,700 flight hours and 380 missions before returning home on 15 December 2008. Despite the Viking's Maverick capability, no Maverick missions were flown over Iraq due the to short notice nature of the deployment and the lack of weapons certification opportunity.

An S-3A with its MAD deployed flies by a U.S. Navy submarine during fleet training exercises. Hunting Soviet submarines was the primary mission of the S-3A. Here, a Checkmate flying from the USS *Saratoga* (CV-60) is seen in high-visibility markings. (Robert Lawson Collection)

A Shadow from VX-1 is readied for a mission aboard USS *Saratoga* (CV-60) during NATO exercise Display Determination '92. VX-1 made the first ES-3A deployment. This photo was taken in the Mediterranean Sea in late September 1992. (LCDR Richard Burgess, USN, [Ret.])

Proof-of-Concept Demonstrators

Although only three S-3 variants were developed, there were several experimental proof-of-concept demonstrators. Proof-of-concept demonstrators were typically the brainchild of the Special Projects Divisions at the Sea Control Wings and involved study of enhancements to the Viking, some resulting from simply off-the-shelf technology. These demonstrators, many of which were based on capabilities that emerged during the 1991 Gulf War, were meant to illustrate the potential for expansion of the Viking's core mission or capabilities in the hope that the modifications could ultimately make their way into fleet service.

Most notable of these demonstrators were Project Gray Wolf and Outlaw Viking, which appeared in 1993 and 1995 respectively. Gray Wolf involved the addition of a stand-off overland tracking and targeting system, which would have given carrier battle group commanders a capability similar to that of the Air Force E-8 JSTARS, performing strike command and control missions and reconnaissance and surveillance of critical mobile targets. The guts of Gray Wolf (BuNo. 158864) consisted of a Norden Systems APG-76 Ku-band (16.5 GHz) radar multi-mode synthetic aperture radar (SAR) with moving target indicator (MTI) housed in a CNU-264/A cargo pod, modified with an F-4 Phantom II nose cone. The APG-76 was developed for the A-6F Intruder and a modified version was planned for Israeli Air Force Phantom IIs (called Kurnass) as part of Phantom 2000.

The Gray Wolf pod was carried on the Viking's right wing station, and was interfaced with a GPS/INS system that aided in targeting accuracy. Information was then transmitted via a secured data link to a ground station monitor. The APS-76 offered several SAR modes, with standard real-beam and Doppler-sharpening modes. Gray Wolf flew with several East Coast squadrons, including VS-22, -24, and -30, and participated in several fleet exercises in the Caribbean and off the Virginia shores. The Gray Wolf program ended, although some of its capabilities were eventually incorporated into the APS-137(V)5 SAR-MTI radar.

Outlaw Viking (BuNo. 160124) demonstrated the ability to utilize over-the-horizon surveillance, targeting, and communications and featured the Over-the-Horizon, Airborne Sensor Information System, called OASIS, developed for the P-3C Outlaw Orion and later adapted as part of the P-3C Update III Anti-surface warfare Improvement Program (AIP). OASIS allowed the integration of the Viking's various sensor systems with a state-of-the-art communications system featuring GPS, SATCOM, and a Link-16 data link. The OASIS gear was operated from the TACCO station, which was modified with a new system interface and a 10-inch liquid crystal display. Physically, a black angled SATCOM antenna positioned on top of the fuselage distinguished Outlaw Viking from regular S-3Bs. Outlaw Viking flew with several squadrons, initially VS-37, and subsequently VS-33, -38, and -29, and had exceptional success, but was eventually retired in the late 1990s for lack of funding.

Other Viking projects had been designed to address specific Navy needs. For instance, during the early 1990s, Lockheed (in conjunction with LTV Aerospace) proposed a

One proposal called for an Airborne Early Warning variant of the S-3, called the AEW Viking. Unlike the E-2C Hawkeye, which used a rotating radome, the AEW Viking would have used electronically phased array radar. (Lockheed Martin via David Reade, P-3 Publications)

Experiments were also conducted by VX-1 using the ALQ-99 jamming pod typically used by the EA-6B Prowler. This modified S-3 belonged to Naval Air Text Center. (LCDR Richard Burgess, USN. [Ret.])

In an unusual mission for any Navy aircraft, on 13 September 1987, FBI agents captured Fawaz Younis, a terrorist charged in the 1985 hijacking and downing of a Jordanian airliner. The FBI transferred Younis to the USS *Saratoga* (CV-60), then stationed in the Mediterranean. He was then flown over 4,000 miles to the United States in a VS-30/CVW-17 S-3A Viking. The 13-hour, 10-minute non-stop flight involved three in-flight refuelings from an Air Force KC-10. Then CDR Phil Voss (center), who later became Commodore of Sea Control Wing, Atlantic Fleet, piloted the Viking, accompanied by a physician and FBI agents. Over CDR Voss' protests, the Viking did not have a navigator or co-pilot. (Commodore Phil Voss, USN, [Ret.])

During the mid-1990s, tests were performed as part of Gray Wolf Project to demonstrate a Synthetic Aperture Radar (SAR) capability. The Westinghouse APG-76 radar was mounted on weapon station 5 in a CNU-296/A cargo pod and fitted with an F-4 Phantom II nose cone. The tests were extremely successful and would have given the Viking a capability comparable to that of the Air Force's larger E-8A JSTARS. However, funding issues ended the program prematurely. (David Reade, P-3 Publications)

West Coast Special Projects created a proof-of-concept and operational flight demonstrator to showcase the application of the P-3C OASIS III system, which had proved successful during the Gulf War. The aircraft, known as Outlaw Viking (BuNo. 160124), initially deployed with VS-37. Outlaw Viking is carrying a Harpoon missile and a range tracking pod (Extended Area Tracking System). (LCDR Kurt Garland)

Viking Airborne Electronic Warfare (AEW) variant to replace the E-2C Hawkeye. The AEW Viking used electronically scanned phased-array radar housed in a triangular-shaped dome atop the fuselage. Another proposal of the early 1990s called for installing a much more sensitive Digital MAD. The Navy installed the AN/ASQ-208 D-MAD on Viking BuNo. 160602 and it operated for several years in exercises in the Caribbean with VS-31 and VS-32. The D-MAD offered 50-percent better detection capabilities, especially in littoral waters and areas of high water temperatures, but the system was not adopted.

Orca Viking was another demonstrator of interest, although it is still denied in some circles. An East Coast program, Orca focused on sonar enhancements, particularly in shallow littoral waters, and involved the installation of an Intrum Extended Echo Ranger (IEER), an advanced sonobuoy receiver, and an ASW laser ranger, as well as a pod-mounted SAR radar based on the Gray Wolf program. Never deployed operationally, Orca provided a test-bed for a system later deployed in the Orion. The West Coast Special Programs worked on their own ASW project called Beartrap. Still classified, Beartrap is said to have deployed with VS-27, but support ended in 1997 due to budget constraints.

Rumors also abound of a classified project, dubbed Aladdin (later known as Arid Hunter), during Operation Deny Flight over Bosnia in late 1993. VS-32 appears to have been involved in the project, as at least one aircraft wore Aladdin titles and drawings on its wing pylons. Stories have conflicted, but some say that the Vikings were involved in dropping overland sensors similar to Vietnam-era Igloo White efforts. Others say these were merely "Brown Buoys" used to deliver materials to Special Forces on the ground.

Sunset for the Viking

The early 2000s marked the beginning of the end for the Viking. With the Navy working to neck-down to three common air wing platforms, namely the F/A-18 E/F Super Hornet and EA-18G Growler, the E-2C Hawkeye, and the HH-60 Seahawk, the Viking's days were numbered. In late 2003, the Navy announced its formal S-3B retirement plan calling for VS squadron complements to reduce from eight to six aircraft upon the air wing's receipt of its first F/A-18E/F squadron, and the eventual retirement of the S-3B squadron upon the receipt of the second Super Hornet squadron.

Official retirement dates were as follows:

VS-29 Dragonfires	30 April 2004
VS-38 Red Griffins	30 April 2004
VS-21 Fighting Red Tails	28 February 2005
VS-35 Blue Wolves	31 March 2005
Sea Control Wing, Pacific	30 September 2006
VS-41 Shamrocks	30 September 2006

A VS-29 Viking heads off into the sunset, signifying the end of 35 years of service. The S-3's mission migrated from that of the lead air wing ASW platform to a true sea control platform. (CAPT Chris Buhlmann, USNR)

An era comes to an end on 30 September 2006, as VS-41 is disestablished. The squadron had been involved in training Viking crews since the aircraft was introduced into the fleet. The squadron had been joined by VS-27, the East Coast FRS, when the S-3B was introduced in 1987, but that squadron was later disestablished in 1994. (United States Navy)

Vidar 703 (BuNo. 160147) prepares for a mission. VS-22, the last operational Viking squadron, held its official disestablish ceremony on 30 January 2009, at NAS Jacksonville, followed the next day by the disestablishment of the Sea Control Wing Atlantic. The Checkmates ended their many years of service flying land-based (ISR) missions out of al-Asad Air Base, al-Anbâr province, Iraq, (a former MiG-25 base known as al-Qâdisîyah before the U.S. invasion of the country in 2003), using the AAQ-25 LANTIRN to monitor Coalition convoys in western Iraq. Four Vidars deployed and accumulated over 1,700 flight hours. Over 80 percent of the squadron's non-traditional intelligence, surveillance, and reconnaissance (NTISR) missions were flown at night. (United States Navy)

On January 29, 2009, disestablishment ceremonies were held for VS-22 *Checkmates* at NAS Jacksonville, followed the next day by Sea Control Wing, Atlantic, bringing an end to the Viking legacy.

Although there were discussions of converting about 20 Vikings to serve the U.S. Coast Guard, the decision was made to use the CASA 142 for that service's medium SAR capability. Four Vikings were taken and modified by NASA for icing testing, and there are plans for three or four to go to VX-30 for range clearance missions.

The S-3 holds a special place in the history of naval aviation. The Viking proved extremely dependable and adaptable to a variety of missions beyond its intended ASW role, and it is one of the few aircraft to be retired from service with over half of its fatigue life still usable. Indeed, the S-3B as it retired in 2009 highlighted the remarkable ability of the Viking to adapt to changing roles and continue its contribution to the Navy's mission, as evidenced by VS-22's NTSIR deployment to Iraq. The Viking ended its long career as a testament to the engineers, designers, and operators who made the aircraft a tremendous success.

One of the Vikings' most serious enemies during its deployment to Iraq in 2008 was the weather. This VS-22 S-3B has its engines, landing gear, and cockpit areas covered with tarps to protect it from sand. (U.S. Navy)

The *Checkmates* ended their many years of service flying land-based (ISR) missions out of al Asad Air Base, Iraq (a former MiG-25 base under Saddam Hussain), using the AAQ-25 LANTIRN to monitor Coalition convoys in western Iraq. Four Vidars deployed and accumulated over 1,700 flight hours. (U.S. Navy)

Two S-3B Vikings assigned to the *Checkmates* of VS-22 sit "chocked and chained" on the flight deck aboard USS *Harry S. Truman* (CVN-75) as a sand storm blew over the Persian Gulf. Carrier Air Wing Three (CVW-3) was providing close air support and conducting intelligence, surveillance and reconnaissance (ISR) missions over Iraq. (U.S. Navy)

Rear Admiral David Architzel attended the decommissioning ceremony for the *Diamond Cutters* of VS-30 on 9 December 2005. The *Diamond Cutters* were the first East Coast S-3B squadron disestablished. (U.S. Navy)

A VS-22 S-3B arrives at Eielson Air Force Base to take part in exercise Red Flag-Alaska, an Air Force level event that enables aviation units to sharpen their combat skills through 10 simulated combat sorties in a realistic threat environment. (U.S. Air Force)

A group of former and present VS-30 Commanding Officers participate in a decommissioning ceremony marking the end of the squadron's legacy with a tombstone ceremony at Naval Air Station Jacksonville. (U.S. Navy)

Three VS-29 Vikings fly in formation. Each is fitted with a refueling store. Aircraft 700 in the foreground wears CAG markings. The *Dragonfires* were commissioned in 1960 and transitioned to the S-3A in 1974. (Ted Carlson, Fotodynamics).

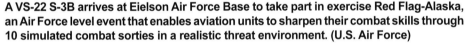

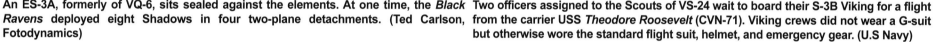

A gathering of 11 S-3Bs can be seen here at the aircraft boneyard at Davis-Monathan AFB. Also shown in this photo are two F-8 Crusaders and seven E-2 Hawkeyes, two with their radar dish removed. (Ted Carlson, Fotodynamics)

LT Zachary Kirby, a pilot assigned to VS-22, watches from the cockpit of his S-3B Viking as sailors on the flight deck try to determine the cause of a wing malfunction responsible for delaying the aircraft's launch aboard USS *Harry S. Truman* (CVN-75). (U.S. Navy)

An ES-3A, formerly of VQ-6, sits sealed against the elements. At one time, the *Black Ravens* deployed eight Shadows in four two-plane detachments. (Ted Carlson, Fotodynamics)

Two officers assigned to the Scouts of VS-24 wait to board their S-3B Viking for a flight from the carrier USS *Theodore Roosevelt* (CVN-71). Viking crews did not wear a G-suit but otherwise wore the standard flight suit, helmet, and emergency gear. (U.S Navy)

The Sea Control Weapons School patch carried the same clout as the Navy Fighter Weapons School "TOPGUN" patch worn by strike fighter crews (Author).

The Viking Weapons Tactics Instructor (WTI) denotes graduates of the Sea Control Weapons School, which was the community's equivalent of the U.S. Navy Fighter Weapons School (TOPGUN). (Author patch; photo by Randall Touckes)

Viking Weapons School

The Viking community enjoyed the support of the Sea Control Weapons School, which was located at NAS Jacksonville, Florida. Prior to 1999 when the East Coast Viking community was based at NAS Cecil Field, the weapons school was part of a joint venture between the VFA and VS communities. But when the Hornets departed for NAS Oceana, Virginia, in 1999, the S-3 community found itself in a dilemma.

In April 1999, the Sea Control Weapons School, Atlantic Fleet (SCWSL) was established as a detachment of the Sea Control Wing, Atlantic Fleet, and given the responsibility of developing and refining tactical doctrine for the Viking community. Using the graduate-level tactical training concepts developed at the Naval Strike and Air Warfare Center (NSAWC) in Fallon, Nevada, the SCWSL quickly sieved the opportunity not only to promote the VS community, but also to take advantage of the close proximity to the VP, HS, and HSL communities located at NAS Jacksonville and nearby NAS Mayport. The SCWSL also provided support to West Coast Viking squadrons through a detachment known as Weapons School Det West, based out of NAS North Island, California.

CDR Timothy "Snake" Summers was the School's first Officer-in-Charge (OIC), serving from its stand-up through 2001. He was followed by CDR Ryman "Skin" Shoaf.

In September 2001, SCWSL was made an echelon-five command and renamed the Sea Control Weapons School (SCWS) for the entire S-3 community. In addition to providing aircrew coordination training, squadron-level simulator training, and conventional weapons proficiency training, SCWS also oversaw two major initiatives from NSAWC – the Sea Control Advanced Readiness Program (SCARP) and the post-FRS air combat training continuum (ACTC). SCARP helped prepare fleet squadrons for the inter-deployment training cycle (IDTC), which was a four-week program culminating in simulated air wing strikes and weapons' deployment. The latter program included the Viking Tactics Instructor (VTI) and ACTC level-five programs, which paralleled TOPGUN's weapons and tactics instructor programs. This program was crucial in ensuring that Viking squadrons maintained a high-level of skills and mission readiness.

In addition to these tasks, SCWS was heavily involved in the development and refinement of Viking tactics and maximum utilization of the Viking in the overall carrier air wing. Viking tactics continually evolved as crews sought to introduce more and more capabilities into the aircraft in order to ensure its significance in carrier air wing operations. As the 2000s progressed, the Viking Weapons School focused more of its efforts on employment of air-to-surface weapons and sensors and less on mining operations. Since 1999, the Viking abandoned its ASW mission, which left the helicopter and Orion squadrons to carry the burden of protecting fleet assets from submarine threats.

During its peak years of operation, SCWS had a staff of 10 officers, 10 enlisted, and two civilian employees and received technical support from as many as 35 contractors. The School played an integral role in the introduction of Viking SSU, Maverick Plus, and SLAM-ER capabilities to the fleet as well as integration of LANTIRN. The School officially closed at the end of 2009.

A wide angle lens captures the view from the Viking cockpit during carrier deck operations. Originally pilots, Viking COTACs were later replaced by NFOs because it was difficult for two pilots to maintain currency and accumulate flight hours. (U.S. Navy)

In 2005, VS-22 deployed aboard USS *Harry S. Truman* (CVN 75). This image shows the aft crew window just behind the "703" Modex. (U.S. Navy)

Shooters signal for a VS-24 Viking to launch from the Number 1 catapult aboard USS *Theodore Roosevelt* (CVN 71). (LI3 Jonathan Snyder, U.S. Navy)

A *Shamrock* Viking leaves the carrier deck on a training mission. VS-41 was responsible for training all West Coast Viking crews and after VS-27 disestablished in the mid-1990s, it trained all Vikings crews (Roland Franklin, U.S. Navy)

An ES-3A Shadow is prepared for a mission. (Ted Carlson, Fotodynamics)

The Viking's clean lines can be seen on this view of a VS-32 aircraft. (Ted Carlson, Fotodynamics)

A Viking from VS-31 *Topcats* is on final approach to the *John C. Stennis* (CVN-74). (U.S. Navy)

This image reflects a pilot's viewpoint of an aerial refueling from another S-3B. The Viking served as the sole tanking asset on U.S. carriers from roughly mid-1990 until the arrival of the Super Hornet in the early 2000s. Vikings were removed from the carrier air wing upon the arrival of the second Super Hornet squadron. (PH3 Joshua Karsten, U.S. Navy)

A VRC-50 US-3A in white markings is seen in this photo (U.S. Navy)

VS-41 officers unveil a memorial to the Viking at NAS North Island honoring Viking squadrons in 2004. At the time of this photo, only VS-33 and VS-41 remained as active West Coast Viking squadrons (PH1 (NAC) Thomas J. Brennan, U.S. Navy)

Six S-3A Vikings were modified as Carrier On-board Delivery (COD) aircraft. The aircraft operated with VRC-50 and with various fleet squadrons. A dedicated COD variant was proposed but never built. (U.S. Navy)

LT Jillene Bushnell, right, salutes her Plane Captain while Rear Admiral Mike Tracy, Commander, Carrier Strike Group Ten (CSG-10), observes from the COTAC's seat. The Viking belongs to VS-22. (U.S. Navy)

An S-3B from VS-33 *Screwbirds,* releases two Mk 83 1,000-lb bombs. The Viking carried out several such attacks during Operation Desert Storm. (CAPT Chris Buhlmann, USNR)

The unmistakable profile of the Viking will always be remembered by naval aviators, NFOs, and aircrew. The Viking began its career as an anti-submarine warfare aircraft and expanded its mission into several areas, including overland reconnaissance, maritime patrol, aerial refueling, ground attack, and targeting. (U.S. Navy).

A Viking from VS-22 is secured to the catapult as the shuttle officer signals "ready." (U.S. Navy)

An Aviation Electronics Technician checks the Aerial Refueling Store (ARS) pod on a VS-35 Viking as it readies for launch from the USS *John C. Stennis* (CVN-74). (U.S. Navy)

An S-3B screams off of the waist catapult. This Viking belongs to VS-30 *Diamondcutters*, which were deployed aboard USS *John F. Kennedy* (CV 67) in late 2004. (PH2 [NAO/SW/AW] Michael Sandberg, U.S. Navy)

An S-3B Viking readies for launch from catapult 4 aboard USS *Enterprise* (CVN-65). The Viking offered tanking services to carrier air wing aircraft. (U.S. Navy)

An ES-3A undergoes maintenance in a hangar at NAS Jacksonville. (Jose Ramos)

A trio of Vikings belonging to VS-29 flies above the Western Pacific *en route* to their carrier, USS *Nimitz* (CVN-68). (U.S. Navy)

Two Vikings from VS-22 demonstrate in-flight refueling with the USS *George Washington* (CVN-73) in the background. The carrier and its air wing were supporting exercises in the Caribbean with the U.S. Southern Command (SOUTHCOM). (U.S. Navy)

Four S-3B Vikings are positioned for launch from catapults 3 and 4 aboard USS *Theodore Roosevelt* (CVN 71). The *Scouts* were assigned to CVW-8 and wear the "AJ" markings. (PHAA Nathan Laird, U.S. Navy)

Three S-3A of VS-29 sit with wings folded and fuel tanks loaded. Vikings were stored with folded wings to conserve deck space. The third Viking's tailfin is folded. (U.S. Navy)

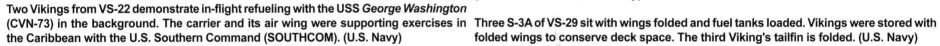

A VS-21 Viking from CVW-5 makes an arrested landing aboard USS *Kitty Hawk* (CV-63). The *Kitty Hawk* was the second to last conventional-powered carrier in the U.S. Fleet and was followed into retirement by USS *Constellation* (CV-64). (U.S. Navy)

Two VS-21 Vikings enter a shallow left bank in formation. The trailing Viking wears the colorful markings of the squadron CAG-aircraft, Modex 700. The *Flying Redtails* were a West Coast squadron forward-deployed to Japan. They were the first West Coast squadron to transition to the S-3B. (U.S. Navy)

The MAD boom of the S-3A/B is replaced by an electronic sensor. Protruding from the aircraft's tail is a long rectangular antenna. (Jose Ramos)

Seen in 2008, this colorful S-3B from VS-22 taxis to one of the carrier's waist catapults. (Jose Ramos)

One Viking prepares to touch down while a second is secured aboard the carrier. Both are configured for aerial refueling and have buddy pods on their left wing. (Jose Ramos)

The first S-3A (BuNo. 157995) makes the type's first carrier landing during initial carrier qualifications. (U.S. Navy)

After landing aboard USS *Theodore Roosevelt* (CVN-71), a Viking from VS-24 folds its wings and prepares to maneuver off of the landing portion of the carrier flight deck. (U.S. Navy)

VS-24 deployed aboard USS *Theodore Roosevelt* (CVN-71) during 2006. Here, the Jet Blast Deflector (JBD) has been raised and a Scout is readied for launch. The left wing holds a refueling store while the right wing carries a fuel tank. (U.S. Navy).

Seen here is a pilot's view of an S-3B receiving fuel from another S-3B. Given the smaller sonobuoy pattern on the VS-29 Viking, this photo was likely taken post-2000. The Viking has had an honorable career spanning four decades and witnessing a mission shift from anti-submarine to full-spectrum sea control and surveillance. (Ted Carlson, Fotodynamics)